holy
and
HUMAN

OVERCOMING SPIRITUAL STRUGGLES
TO LIVE A HOLY LIFE

EARLE L. WILSON
Th.B., B.D., Th.M., D.D.

wesleyan
publishing
house

Indianapolis, Indiana

Copyright © 2008 by Wesleyan Publishing House
Published by Wesleyan Publishing House
Indianapolis, Indiana 46250
Printed in the United States of America
ISBN: 978-0-89827-355-7

Library of Congress Cataloging-in-Publication Data

Wilson, Earle L.
  Holy and human : overcoming spiritual struggles to live a holy life /
Earle L. Wilson.
    p. cm.
  ISBN 978-0-89827-355-7
  1. Spirituality. 2. Christian life. I. Title.
  BV4501.3.W5544 2008
  248.4--dc22
                                        2008018530

All Scripture quotations, unless otherwise indicated, are taken from the HOLY
BIBLE, NEW INTERNATIONAL VERSION ®. NIV ®. Copyright 1973, 1978, 1984 by
the International Bible Society. Used by permission of Zondervan. All rights
reserved.

Scripture quotations marked (KJV) are taken from THE HOLY BIBLE, King JAMES
VERSION.

All rights reserved. No part of this publication may be reproduced, stored in a
retrieval system, or transmitted in any form or by any means—electronic,
mechanical, photocopy, recording or any other—except for brief quotations in
printed reviews, without the prior written permission of the publisher.

CONTENTS

INTRODUCTION

The day you became a believer, when Christ came into your life and changed you, was the day the new race began. No longer trapped in the world's meaningless rat race, you are running toward the promise of the finish line, to hear your Lord proclaim, "Well done!"

At that first crack of the starter's gun, when God's Holy Spirit entered into your life, you took off with fresh fire. Now that you've started to find your stride, you find energy waning. Obstacles are popping up along the way. You begin to wonder: Do I have what it takes—God's sufficient grace—to see this race through?

We have all struggled with this conflict—it seems at the core of our beings. We are loathe to acknowledge it, yet there is no escaping the hard reality that what we believers expect God's grace to do for us is a far stretch from what His grace is and does, at least as far as our day-to-day living is concerned.

There is often a disconnect between what we think we should believe and what God is actually doing. It was our faith that reached out to those grace promises and embraced wonderful spiritual realities: forgiveness by God, cleansing through His Word, healing by His touch, and strength by His Holy Spirit. For good reason we were encouraged as new converts to believe largely, expect broadly, and hope eternally—to win big!

But as inevitable as any marathon runner's midcourse battle, we eventually run into spiritual walls, made of the often-painful realities of life. When we hit those walls, we face a range of human emotions that can bring us into conflict with our newfound faith. Before we can say "Hallelujah," inconsistencies start popping up, causing us to question the level of grace we received—"maybe God hamstrung me." When the wall looms larger than ever, threateningly, and inconceivably, Christ starts to seem distant, remote from the daily grind of life.

As difficult as this moment is, it is a test of endurance we should be anticipating and welcoming. For this is the time when we learn to define our humanness as we live the Christian life. Simplistic, shallow answers will not cut it. Cheap psychology, quick cures, pie-in-the-sky promises, head-in-the-sand tactics are of no avail. What we need in order to run through the wall is to discover personally the resources only God's Word can provide.

In my years of pastoral ministry and institutional leadership, I've watched a lot of young Christian runners pass through. Many have reminded me there is a great chasm between what we expect grace to do for us and what God's grace is about. Many of us know we need help with our behavioral issues. But more fundamentally, we all must face the emotions that drive our behavior.

In this book I draw upon my sermon preparation and preaching experience to deal with those human emotions that weigh us down. I hope to bring you encouragement and strength, to press through the spiritual walls, and to show that the conflicts we all experience as we attempt to be honest with both God and ourselves are not unusual, should not be surprising, and need not be faith diminishing.

As you read, you will be introduced to runners of the past whose races are recounted in the Bible. They have faced the same human emotions you are facing. They triumphed, and so can you.

You also will run alongside believers whom I have met on the road of life—contemporary marathoners who experienced the tough battles, made the difficult choices, and were successful in their journeys. You can be, too.

Each chapter can stand alone, so you may turn to any relevant emotion independently. I could not hope to map out every nuance of every emotion within these pages; but by finding our stride through some of the major obstacles, we will build confidence by reinforcing the truth that God's grace is compatible with our humanity.

My purpose is to introduce you to enough people and circumstances to give you confidence in your experience with God. Likewise you should find sufficient practical coaching to press through and endure inevitable obstacles. The road you travel is the one we all travel, though not at the same time or the same pace. You do not face any emotion that has not been faced, to some degree, by all who travel the well-worn road.

My prayer is that you will experience God's grace that not only triumphs over all sin, but that also enables the Christian to live serenely and confidently in a world of sin and strain.

"Therefore, since we are surrounded by such a great cloud of witnesses, let us throw off everything that hinders and the sin that so easily entangles, and let us run with perseverance the race marked out for us" (Heb. 12:1).

1

BEATING FRUSTRATION

Frustrated plans are unavoidable;
Christ calls us to persevere by focusing on Him.

To leave unseen so many a glorious sight,
To leave so many lands unvisited,
To leave so many worthy books unread,
Unrealized so many visions bright.
Oh! Wretched yet inevitable spite
Of our brief span, that we must yield our breath,
And wrap us in the unfeeling coil of death,
So much remaining of unproved delight.

—Author unknown

Frustrated hope, unrealized dreams—in this we are all alike, we all meet on the common ground of the experience of frustration. The question is not whether we will face frustrations, but *how* we will deal with the frustrations we are sure to face. Is there a godly way to manage our frustrations? The answer to this question is crucial for the believer.

THE BEST-LAID PLANS

Your frustrations are personal and deeply felt; only our heavenly Father knows what you will face tomorrow. None can know exactly what you are going through, but I do know life has a way of bringing a variety of frustrations to each of us. As unique as our frustrations are, they fall into typical categories. Realizing these can help us better understand our struggles.

UNREALIZED HOPES

Many frustrations are attached to specific plans or hopes. It happens like this. You decide on a course of action. Having made that decision, your hopes for the fruition of that plan are born. But somehow, the way is blocked. Perhaps you'd planned a cherished project, only to have the project rejected. You set out toward the open door that promises the fulfillment of your dreams, and life cruelly slammed the door shut. Here is a man who dreams of traveling the world, yet he seems destined to remain in an office. Or here is a woman engaged to be married, but her sweetheart never comes home from the war.

We've all felt it—that beating of the wings from the eternal spirit within, trying to break free, pounding against the bars of irksome limitations: hampering circumstances; life's limitations; physical, intellectual, or social frustrations.

It was my privilege for a few years to study at Princeton Theological Seminary. The seminary is a part of the larger campus of Princeton University. In that university and in that seminary reside two of the greatest libraries in the world. Often I would sit in one of those libraries reading, studying. More often than not I would think of all the books filling hundreds and thousands of shelves—books I would never have opportunity or time to read. All that vast store of knowledge, I shall never acquire in this life.

LIFE'S SHORTFALLS

Some of the frustrations of life center in and revolve around character issues. How splendid the brave resolves we often make; how pathetic and disappointing the reality. The apostle Paul knew this frustration firsthand: "For what I do is not the good I want to do; no, the evil I do not want to do—this I keep on doing" (Rom. 7:19). The question all honest Christians will ask themselves is: "Why can't I reproduce the love, trust, and selflessness of Jesus fully in my life?"

Beyond our personal shortcomings, there is another range of frustrations we all carry at times—the frustrations of our dreams for our world. When World War I was raging, humanity assured itself this was the war to end all wars: *We will never make the same mistakes again. We will set ourselves to build a wonderful new temple of brotherhood and humanity.* When the war was over, what happened? World War II. And after that the world continued with heaving unrest, wars, and the perpetual estrangement of suspicion.

No wonder our youth are discontented. We keep promising them a utopia of goodwill that will break like a new dawn upon the human race, yet they only see that dream sabotaged and wrecked. Every generation asks, "Must we always be frustrated in our desire to build the ideal society?" And the response is always the same: perpetual frustration.

While it's not much consolation, all of us know frustration in many ways—individual, general, and of a world scope. Cold comfort as it may be, it's important to have the perspective that you are not alone in this burden. It is common to all mankind—it's the human condition.

FRUSTRATION OF BIBLICAL PROPORTIONS

Take a walk with me through Bible times. Again and again within the Word of God, you will find men and women wrestling with the same frustrating problems we bear.

FRUSTRATED SAINTS OF OLD

Moses: After four decades of desert wandering, here he finally stands on Mount Pisgah, looking across the Jordan at the Promised

Land. For all those weary years, this had been his heart's longing, his life's purpose—the Canaan of his dreams, the land flowing with milk and honey.

"O Lord," he cries, "let me go over; let me tread the good land beyond the Jordan. I have waited for this for forty years. Will You refuse me now? Let me go over."

But God's reply is final. "Enough. Ask me no more. Speak not of this again." And there, within sight of the goal he has struggled toward through half a lifetime, he dies in the desert, shut out, frustrated. (See Deut. 3:23–29.)

Jeremiah: Called by God to be a prophet and a preacher, he starts with the dream of an Israel reborn, but as the years go by he encounters baffling indifference, unimaginative stolidity, and the hostility of his people. "O Lord, You have deceived me, and I was deceived," he laments. Bitter frustration; his great dream is gone.

Paul: He has great plans to launch a campaign in Bithynia, on the shores of the Black Sea. He dreams of an Asiatic empire for Christ. We can only wonder what modern Russia would be like had he gone there. But the providence of God confounds his strategy, bars the door against his entrance, drives him off another way—frustrated.

Generations of Jews: Theirs was the dream of a New Jerusalem. As the writer of Hebrews celebrates bygone heroes, he recalls that the common inspiration of those men and women of every age was the unfulfilled vision of the restored city. It drove them out as pilgrims and sojourners, urging and luring them on. "All these people were still living by faith when they died. They did not receive the things promised" (Heb. 11:13). Not one of them attained the Zion of their hopes. They were frustrated.

David: The great leader of the Old Testament, a man after God's own heart, illustrates one of the more tragic instances of frustration. All his life it had been David's firm and settled intention to give God a home in the heart of Zion, to erect in Jerusalem a shrine to be the focus of the national faith and the goal of a thousand and more pilgrimages. As one unknown poet expressed it:

> To this the joyful nations round,
> All tribes and tongues shall flow;
> 'Up to the hill of God,' they'll say,
> And to His house we'll go.

Even in the heat and fury of war, even when disaster had driven him an outlaw from the throne, this high hope flamed within his soul. He proclaimed:

> I will allow no sleep to my eyes,
> no slumber to my eyelids,
> till I find a place for the LORD,
> a dwelling for the Mighty One of Jacob. . . .
> arise, O LORD, and come to your resting place,
> you and the ark of your might. . . .
> For the sake of David your servant,
> do not reject your anointed one. . . .
> For the LORD has chosen Zion,
> he has desired it for his dwelling (Ps. 132:4–13).

Now, at last, the wars were over. The land was bathed in the sunshine of prosperity and peace. The way seemed clear, and with all his characteristic fervor David set himself to the realization of his ideal—to the translating of that dream into the magnificent structure to become the crowning achievement of his reign and the glory of Mount Zion forever.

But God said, "No, you shall not build the temple. Other hands shall build it when you are dead and gone" (see 1 Kings 8:19 and

2 Chron. 6:9). We can only imagine the heartbreaking frustration he must have felt.

DO WELL IN YOUR HEART

There may be comfort in knowing we are not alone in our frustrations. However, the questions remain: How are we to discover meaning through such experiences? Is there a divine adjudication in our frustrations? Does God have anything to say to us? If so, what?

We know what God said to David. We should mark it well, for it is a flash of light across the darkness of many painful enigmas. From God's encounter with David we learn it is a great thing to have a vision, even if your eyes never see its fulfillment. "Because it was in your heart to build a temple for my Name, you did well to have this in your heart" (1 Kings 8:18).

Remember David's life was a rather checkered one. It had its splendor, but it had its sin; its glory, but also its shame. God never looks lightly on sin and the shame attached to it. Contrary to popular opinion, God does not close His eyes to sin.

Yet here is the comforting word as it was expressed in David's case. According to God's word to David, the most important thing in David's life was his abiding vision—his passion to build a house in which the honor of the Lord would dwell. Over that fact God spoke to David: "You did well."

So is it just the thought that counts? Does that mean that we may glorify good intentions, and with that God will be pleased? There are people who have good things in their heart which they would like to do, but they never do them.

You can make your own list of such good intentions. Here are some common ones:

- I will visit that sick friend, someday.
- I will write that important letter, someday.

- I will make that restitution, someday.
- I will get right with God, someday.

Meanwhile, we drift on, never acting on the intended good. Saint Augustine was like this for a while in his young life. He heard a voice calling, "Awake, you that are asleep and arise from the dead, and Christ will give you light." And he drowsily murmured, "Yes, presently; leave me for a little while." He even prayed, "O God make me pure, but not yet."

It will be a tragic distortion of this Scripture related to David to suggest that good intentions are all God requires. What it is saying is, *Do not let the world's standard of success define your vision nor rob you of your dreams.*

To this day, we have not yet been able to build that long wished-for temple of the Most High God. We are far from an earth of justice and equality—from social justice, righteousness, and brotherhood. Where is our temple to the honor of the God of peace and love? We have not yet built that. But it will be a terrible day for humanity if we lose the driving hope of it; if we allow the frustrations we have experienced to beat us into cynicism and despair.

The world calls us unrealistic visionaries. "If only these Christians would come down to earth," they say. They taunted Christ the same way: "Let him come down now from the cross, and we will believe in him" (Matt. 27:42). But Jesus preached a kingdom that was not a success story, but rather the bearing of a cross. That is because His vision was to do His Father's will.

For good reason, youth are disillusioned with the world we have given them. They are resorting to drugs and false sexuality, desperately trying to escape the gnawing vacuum in their lives.

TRUE VISION

We must not allow the bitter realities to rob us of our vision. We know the church has not built the kingdom of God as we would like to build it. We haven't eliminated racial hatred and social evils. The world temple of righteousness and peace does not yet stand. But let us not lose heart. Let us work and believe that salvation can still girdle this globe.

It would be a death blow to civilization if the Christians take the pessimistic attitude of despair that has characterized our age. It would be a supreme disloyalty to Christ. We still have a vision for changing society; for bettering humanity; for building the temple. Yes, we are frustrated in our attempts to build a better society. But God says to us, "'Because it was in your heart . . . you did well."

What is true of our frustration with the world is also true of our individual lives. Most of us have not come as near as we should like to building a life that truly imitates Christ. If we should have a day when we lose the inspiration of that high intention, God have mercy on us.

Remember the challenge in Hebrews? "Let us run with perseverance the race marked out for us" (12:1). Verse 2 goes on to explain, "Let us fix our eyes on Jesus, the author and perfecter of our faith." Our inspiration and means of sustaining that high intention is keeping our eyes on Jesus. And God's Word promises He will perfect and He will sustain our faith. After all, He is the author of it.

There is a marvelous text, Micah 7:8, which John Bunyan used most dramatically in the description of his Pilgrim's terrible fight with Apollyon. Christian, thrown again and again by Apollyon, is struggling doggedly and indomitable at his feet. He is crying, "Rejoice not against me, O mine enemy: when I fall, I shall arise." Life must not rob us of that.

There are moods and voices that come to us tauntingly, saying, "You call yourself a follower of Jesus? You aim at Christlikeness?

You dream of building your life into a temple of the Lord. How absurd." Yes, it may be folly; but be a fool for Christ's sake. Keep the hope in your heart. Perhaps you fall short of His glory too often. Perhaps you are frustrated because you are a human being. Even though you can rejoice in the ground you have gained, like Israel you know there is more to possess, and you shall never possess it all here.

Keep the vision on Jesus.

FACING JESUS' DIRECTION

This is what the New Testament calls "justification by faith." That means a person's relationship to the kingdom of Christ is not defined by some point he has reached on the highway of holiness, but by the direction he is facing. Justification is not measured by the distance of the pilgrimage, but by the direction of his life. Not by the question, "Has he achieved a complete and perfect character?" but by the question, "Has he set his face to Christ, or his back?"

The perfect ideal of Christlikeness will never be attained in this life, but the ideal must always be there. The most important thing about the Christian life is not the attainment but the aspiration. This is why I don't think you should be too interested in how much grace you have obtained, or even how far you are toward Christ. Your interest rather should be in knowing which direction you are headed. Are you on the way?

We are frustrated at times in building an ideal society and an ideal Christian life. It is then we must remember what God said to David: keep the vision; do not allow the frustration to turn you from the path.

TURNING YOUR FRUSTRATION OVER TO GLORY

Note how David capitalized on his disappointed desire and turned that frustration to gain. He could have become rebellious. Many do when up against a great disappointment. How easy it is to become bitter; to allow our nerves to be on edge; to rail against divine providence; to become angry at God's government of the world.

Others attempt to tamper with divine purposes and declare, "I will have my own way; I will cut a pathway clear across the decree of heaven; I am determined to get what I want." Such people push and shove and become rude with those around them. They are the bullies of earth who trample on the rights of others and curse God either by word or attitude, or both. David did not choose these paths. If his heart's desire were to elude him forever, if the dominant desires of his life were never to be fulfilled, so be it—God's will be done.

"I refuse to be disappointed," wrote missionary James Hannington, when bitter opposition was wrecking his dreams for Africa. "I will only praise." The person who speaks like that transcends frustration.

David did more than acquiesce. He knew he would never build the temple, but he could spend the rest of his life preparing the task for those who would come after him. Lesser men might have said, "If I am not to build the temple, I will do nothing about it at all. I have no more interest." But David's attitude was, "What can I do now to help the future generation to which this great achievement will belong?"

We know what he did. From all over the land he gathered expert craftsmen; he amassed materials; he arranged contracts for stone, timber, iron and silver; he laid foundations. With all his strength he toiled for the temple God told him he would never see.

LAYING A FOUNDATION

God's people react that way. Missionaries have sacrificed themselves and died without a name in history for remembrance, all so others might build upon their dust a living temple to the Lord. As the psalmist declares, they have gone "out weeping, carrying seed to sow" (126:6), so the next generation might reap a harvest. Where did they learn that? From the Lord Christ who did precisely that on Calvary.

Lord, cries the great poet of Psalm 90, "May your deeds be shown to your servants, your splendor to their children" (v 16). Give the work to us; the glory to our children. Give us the sacrifice, the discipline, the unfinished symphony, the frustrated hope, but give them, our children, the nobler heritage, the kindlier world.

That is the way to be victorious over frustration. Work on and on and on, so God's glory may be shown to those who follow. When the magnificent sanctuary stood complete, at last, on Mount Zion, men called it Solomon's temple, but it was also David's achievement. Solomon never could have done it if David had not prayed, sacrificed, toiled, and kept God's vision constantly before his eyes.

The Bible speaks of people who "were still living by faith when they died. They did not receive the things promised; they only saw them and welcomed them from a distance" (Heb. 11:13). What we have today, in the church, is not ours but their achievement. So what if we cannot build the temple; as we see it only "from a distance," let us make sure they shall have a foundation on which to build.

KINGDOM PATRIOTS

There is a moving letter oft quoted by distinguished war correspondent Alan Moorhead. It is a letter a Yugoslav patriot, not knowing he was about to die, wrote to his unborn son. Here are the closing sentences.

Now I know I must die and you must be born to stand on the rubbish heap of my errors. Forgive me for this. I am ashamed to leave you an untidy, uncomfortable world. But so it must be. In thought, as a last benediction, I kiss your forehead. Goodnight to you and good morning, and a clear dawn.

So speaks the patriot to his child unborn. There is another, even more noble patriotism, the patriotism of the kingdom of Jesus Christ. "If I forget you, O Jerusalem, may my right hand forget its skill. Walk about Zion, go around her, count her towers, consider well her ramparts, view her citadels, that you may tell of them to the next generation" (Ps. 139:5; 48:12–13).

Looking down the future generations and dreaming of a fairer world that will be the temple of the Lord, we too would say to the generations coming after us, "You have to stand on the rubbish heap of our errors. Forgive us for this." But, we believe in God. Christ has kindled in us the dream of a kingdom that cannot die. For the coming of that kingdom we pledge our toil and prayers and sacrifice until our day on earth is done. What matter if we must pass away? His kingdom cannot fail; His temples rise in glory at last. The whole world shall be His dwelling place one day. Therefore, we wish you, in Christ's Name, a good morning and a clear dawn.

Indeed, we stand on the rubbish heap of our errors. We are often ashamed of the untidy mess of our efforts to live for Christ. But we believe that one day we shall be like Him, for we shall see Him as He is.

Frustrations? Yes, but our eyes are on Jesus. Out of such unlikely raw materials as ourselves, our Lord promises to fulfill a gold morning and a clear dawn.

2

FINDING GOOD IN
DISAPPOINTMENTS

The most noble plans often culminate in disappointment;
We can win through recognizing God's guiding hand in changed direction.

The apostle Paul wanted to go to Spain. He had his heart set on going there. He believed it was God's will for him to go to this land that had not yet heard the gospel. In his letter to the Romans, he all but promises it will happen:

> But now that there is no more place for me to work in these regions, and since I have been longing for many years to see you, I plan to do so when I go to Spain. I hope to visit you while passing through and to have you assist me on my journey there, after I have enjoyed your company for a while. . . . So after I have completed this task and have made sure that they have received this fruit, I will go to Spain and visit you on the way (15:23–24, 28).

He never made it.

Instead of Spain, he got a prison cell in Rome. One can only imagine the depth of his disappointment in having this noble plan frustrated by the circumstances of life.

Paul's experience has something to say to us. Along the road of life all of us will have to deal with disappointment, disrupted plans, deferred hope, and unrealized dreams. Every person's life is a diary in which he or she intends to write one story, but is forced to write another.

Our understanding of God's grace teaches that Christ did not come to reduce life, but to fulfill it—that we might have life more abundantly (see John 10:10). Since desire is one of the major driving forces of life, Christ likewise did not come not to eliminate human desire, but to dedicate and fulfill it. But what happens when human desires are not fulfilled? What happens when our dearest, legitimate hopes and dreams are frustrated? What is God's answer to life's severe disappointments?

Paul is a powerful example of a godly Christian life and yet, as we've seen, his earnest desire was never fulfilled. Paul attests to the reality that in this world, anyone unprepared for such a joust with disappointment is not really conditioned for life. We dream and pray for our personal version of Spain, and yet at times all we experience is imprisoning disappointment of life in a fallen world. If Christ cannot speak to us at this level, He has nothing to say to us at all.

WHEN LIFE WON'T SUBMIT TO YOUR WILL

Modern psychology is telling us that the increase in suicides, alcoholism, even some forms of nervous breakdowns is evidence that many people are training for success, when pragmatically they should be preparing for failure. Obviously, failure is more common than success; poverty is more prevalent than wealth; disappointment more the norm than arrival.

Despite what the world's media preaches to us, we are not guaranteed to acquire all of our hearts' desires, nor attain all of our dreams, no matter how hard we work at it. One key reason is because we are not gods of our universes—there is one true God, whose will always supersedes ours. For those who were banking on being sovereign over their own little worlds, that alone is disappointing. Despite appearances portrayed by rich and famous folk, none of us has the chance to live life on the basis of our choice. Even though some will experience moments and occasions of apparent success (when their will would seem to coincide with God's), all of us must settle for something less than we want.

If we are not prepared for anything but success, if we have no philosophy of failure, we are not ready to face the most normal issues of life. "When I go to Spain," wrote Paul, yet he never took that journey. Instead he journeyed to Rome, and there he sat in prison, scribbling on a bit of parchment.

RESISTANCE THAT'S NOT FUTILE

Authentic Christianity not only demonstrates its superiority to other world religions in its great plan of redemption, including its concept of deity and the infinite worth of each person; it also is superior in how it faces life's disappointments. Christianity responds to life's tragic elements redemptively.

This is because Christianity was born in the fires of failure and defeat. Its symbol is a cross on which its Founder took the worst in the world and transformed it into an instrument of redemption. A core meaning of the cross and our faith is that grace was forged in the fires of profound human disappointment. Even the worst the world has to offer may be a blessing for those who trust in God (see Rom. 8:28).

No one would seek out or pretend to enjoy pain. Yet without pain there would be little progress. It is the disappointment that can often give us the best traction. Even biologically, all life makes progress in a resisting medium. The bird needs the resistance of the air to fly; the fish needs the resistance of the water for its fins to propel it forward.

WHEN GOD WEIGHS US DOWN

An old grandfather clock stood in the corner of a room for three generations, faithfully ticking the minutes, the hours, the days. Its momentum came from a heavy weight suspended by a double chain.

"Too bad," thought the new owner, one day. "Too bad such an old clock must bear such a great load." So he released the weight and took it out. The ticking stopped.

"Why did you do that?" asked the clock.

"I wanted to lighten your burden," replied the owner.

"Please," said the clock, "put back my weight; it is the weight that keeps me going."

Life's troubles can be so disagreeable, the weight of them so heavy, that we never see them as components God has installed into our lives for our own help. Most of us looking back on our lives would have to admit that whatever gain there has been in terms of character has come through conflict. It has come to us through God's power deep within—the power of His Holy Spirit. God uses the weights of life to keep His people going.

FINDING COMFORT

At this point much popular Christianity misses the point. The cults of comfort are in error. Anyone who is telling us, either within the church or outside it, that we must dodge pain and trouble by metaphysical gymnastics, or think it away by simply believing—anyone who proposes in this fallen world a reality that could be all pleasure with no pain, is mistaken.

These light, easy answers are based on the false assumption that the goal of life is self-made happiness, peace of mind, and comfort. Despite common sensibilities, that is not the goal, nor the meaning of human existence. Holiness, not happiness, is the goal of life, because that alone is how one can gain true happiness. We were created for holiness—to be in right and intimate relationship with God. But when sin entered human existence, we were separated from God. This is why we cannot hope to have true happiness until that unholy divide is repaired.

That is why when God molds a believer, He puts weights on that person. He gives him or her burdens to lift, crosses to carry, hardships to endure, tribulations over which to triumph. He uses those weights to mold lives into holy images of Christ.

Only for those of us who are in Christ can pain truly have purpose, can frustrations be fruitful, and can weights keep us going. Christianity faces disappointments and crosses head-on, because followers of Christ are promised His same outcome—the Father will exult, He will bring justice, and He will fulfill. So He does not promise an easy release from them. In fact, Christianity paradoxically points to failure as the proving ground of God's grace, evidenced most dramatically by Calvary.

TOUGH BREAKS, TOUGHER SPIRIT

Life is full of accidental frustrations, when it can seem as though blind fate were in control, spinning the wheel of fortune. "A tough break," we call it.

Many people go through life broken by tough breaks. They invest a fortune, but the bottom falls out of the stock market. They take up a life task, but health fails. They want marriage, but find the door is closed by family responsibilities they cannot disregard. How can Christ deal redemptively with such? How can failing be fruitful?

There was once a boy in Decatur, Illinois, became deeply interested in photography. He answered an advertisement in a magazine and sent twenty-five cents for a book on photography. The publishers, however, made a mistake with his order and sent him instead a *Manual on Magic, Mind-reading and Ventriloquism*. The chapter on ventriloquism fascinated the young Swedish lad, and he began practicing by throwing his voice. You who are older have probably heard of him. He created a wooden dummy to whom, at one time, more people listened on Sunday night than to all the preachers on the continent. That was Edgar Bergen and his little friend, Charlie McCarthy.

In 1915, Coffee County, Alabama, was a starving community in the cotton belt. The cotton had been invaded by the boll weevil, which stripped the plants of their leaves and stole the people's livelihood. When it seemed hopeless, people began listening to a young scientist named George Washington Carver. He told them to turn from cotton to peanuts. In the lowly peanut he had found unbelievable riches: chemicals for soap, ink, paper, plastics, even shampoo. So in 1919 the people of Coffee County, on their way to becoming a prosperous community, erected a memorial. The inscription reads, "In profound appreciation of the boll weevil and of what it has done as the herald of prosperity, this monument is erected by the citizens of Enterprise, Coffee County, Alabama."

Thomas Edison, selling newspapers in a western railroad, was fired because he spilled acid in a baggage car and set it on fire. The accident turned him to scientific research. What a fruitful blunder. Victor Hugo was banished by the German emperor at the age of forty-eight. On the isle of his loneliness he wrote his greatest works. "I should have been banished earlier," he said.

GOD INTENDED IT FOR GOOD

The prophet Hosea saw similar irony centuries before when he spoke of the Valley of Achor, that fearful valley in which was buried the thief Achan, whose treacherous disobedience resulted in Israel's bitter defeat at the hands of Ai. The site became the synonym of despair and disgrace. But through Hosea the Lord promised His people He would "make the Valley of Achor a door of hope" (2:15).

So, where is the Achor of your life? Where is your valley of despair? Or like Paul, have you missed your Spain only to get a prison? It's disappointing to say the least, but it does not necessarily mean the end of everything. It may, in fact, be the beginning of something greater than you ever imagined.

In the New Testament there are fourteen letters of Paul, making up the bulk of the Testament. Most of those letters were written while Paul was in jail. Some of the best would not have been written if Paul had gone to Spain as he wished. It's hard to escape the conclusion then that God was orchestrating that disappointment, giving Paul a prison cell from which to pour forth those great words of immortal hope and faith. Out of Paul's frustration in not reaching Spain came some of the greatest contributions of his life.

Pain can be profitable; disappointments can be fruitful. This is a sound and good philosophy by which even many pragmatic secularists will face life. But is it necessarily Christian?

Let's face it, not all our failings will turn into good fortune. Some of them we have to live with endlessly. Not all our prisons open out on the centuries. Some of them are dark and dreary places. They are made of great, impenetrable walls, shutting in the spirit and leaving it to beat in vain against the bars. To what end? To live on with a broken body? a broken heart? a broken home? When the disappointment settles into the chronic, the pernicious, what then?

For many of us, it's only then that we finally will go deeper than the magazine success stories, deeper than the surface philosophies. Then can we go into the profound underlying meaning of the cross.

THE POWER TO GAIN THROUGH PAIN

Tolstoy was a great Russian philosopher. He became a strong Christian. In his book, *My Confessions* he described how most people, left to their own means, will face tragedy, disappointment, and defeat:

- those who are frightened by the dire turn of events and go out and get drunk;
- those who give way to despair and commit suicide;
- those who resent the hard blows of life and stoically steel themselves against them and harden their hearts; and
- those who irrationally accept life as it comes, yet stand up bravely to it.

Tolstoy listed himself with the last group.

Is that the best life has to offer? When the tragic elements of life come, must we just grin and bear them? Are we left merely to courageously endure life?

At this point Christianity flexes its muscles. Christ passes all of humanity's feeble answers to life's defeats and tragedies. Although there is some good in a few of them, they all leave out the one key creative element: redemption.

It runs all through the New Testament, the cross of Christ its supreme symbol and illustration. Jesus did not merely "endure the cross"; He used it to redeem. He didn't merely bear the blows that life hurled at Him; He took them, redeemed them, and made them weapons against evil.

Out of the shame, isolation, and unfathomable pain of the cross, He provided salvation for the world. He took the fierce winds that beat against Him and made them a force to lift men and women to the feet of God. "And from the ground there blossoms red, life that shall endless be."

Christ's answer to disappointment is that through Him, adversity must be made to pay dividends—to put into one's life a richness that wasn't there before. "Out of the eater, something to eat; out of the strong, something sweet" riddled Samson, referring to his battle with a lion (Judg. 14:14). He had discovered that bees lived in the carcass of the lion he had slain, producing honey—sweetness out of death, even. Indeed, through God's power, adversity is transformed into the status of a servant of spiritual achievement. God alone can make every disappointment, every broken hope, every severed relationship pay a profit.

The cross means that we should get something out of everything, even out of our defeats. If you missed your Spain and got a prison, the redemptive question is not, "How can I bear this thing?" Rather it should be, "How can I use it in a positive way to God's glory?"

You may never get out of the pain or failure, but you can get *something* out of it—something to make life better for someone else and to turn the disappointment into achievement. The cross means more than this, but it does also mean this: it stands forever as a symbol of victory over the worst the world can do.

WOUNDED HEALER

Thornton Wilder once wrote a three-minute drama titled "An Angel That Troubled the Waters," based on the gospel story of the pool of Bethesda. The chief character is a doctor who is sick with a wound he cannot heal. Along with the other sick people around the pool, he stands waiting for the stirring of the waters that he may get in first and be made whole.

But the angels stand there saying, "Draw back physician, healing is not for you. Without your wound, where would your healing be? It is your very sorrow that puts kindness in your face and makes your low voice tremble into the hearts of men. The angels themselves cannot heal the wretched as can one human being broken on the wheel of life. In love's service, only the wounded can serve."

So in disappointment the physician turns away to live with his wound, never to be cured. But even as he turns, a man comes crying to him, "Come home with me, sir, if only for an hour. My son is lost in dark thoughts; no one understands him and only you have ever lifted his mood. My daughter, since her child died, sits in the shadow; she will not listen to us. Only you, who are wounded, can help her."

Perhaps you will have to live with some cross. Perhaps there will be no miracle to make it easy for you; no angel to help you out of it. But, because you belong with the wounded, the people who sit in a shadowland will turn to you for that intangible something that puts hope into life.

FORTUNATE FAULTS

Up in the north of Scotland is a hunting lodge that has become a showplace. One day, years ago, a guest opened a bottle of liquid and splashed its contents over the newly decorated wall. The other guests hoped it would dry and in drying disappear, but it did not. It left a long unsightly splotch, stretching almost from floor to ceiling. The host was frustrated, and the guests went away feeling the scolding of their host was justified.

But one man remained behind. He studied the blotch on the wall and then went to work on it with crayon and charcoal and finally with oil paints. With quick, bold strokes he turned the brown stains into highland rocks with a cataract pouring over them. Where the stain was deep he painted a glorious highland stag leaping into the torrent, pursued by hunters in the background. His name? Sir Edwin Landseer, the artist famous for his paintings of animals. By his thoughtful and considerate action, he brought beauty out of ugliness.

Ever since, every artist passing through the town has stopped to study Landseer's picture, and on the wall of that lodge many great artists have added drawings of their own. Now it is no longer just a hunting lodge for careless guests, but an abiding place for creativity and an art museum for those who love beauty.

Abraham Lincoln tried to reach the heights as a lawyer and failed. At age forty-six he considered himself the consummate failure of his time and almost by coincidence turned in the direction that led him to the White House.

James McNeill Whistler, the artist, wanted to be a soldier but failed in his chemical examination at West Point. He often chuckled over that, noting that "if silicon had been a gas, I would have been a major general." The world of artistic beauty can be thankful for his personal disappointment and failure.

John Wesley wanted to be a missionary. He came to Georgia to convert the American Indians, failed miserably and went back to England a defeated man. But out of the disappointing defeat he found personal salvation and a great church movement was born.

THE POWER IN BUDDY'S WHEELCHAIR

When I was a boy I spent two weeks every summer at a quaint campground between the great cities of Albany and Schenectady, New York. My parents had a two-room cabin on that campground where, for those few days each year, we washed with water in a little basin and slept, all seven of us, in lumpy, smelly beds. We listened to fiery preachers and emotional music.

There I met "Buddy" Hardy. Buddy suffered from polio and was a paraplegic. He would come to that camp with his parents. We became friends. He was confined to his wheelchair. He lifted his right arm by biting a piece of cloth sewn to his sleeve and lifting his arm with his teeth. I would help him stand just to change his position. I pushed him in his wheelchair around the campgrounds and into the old tabernacle.

He confided that he believed that when he was sixteen God would heal him, his useless legs would be made whole, and he would stand. His twisted arms would be straightened and strengthened, and he would be able to lift them and use them without pulling on his sleeve with his teeth. Buddy lived for his sixteenth birthday, for he was certain that during the camp that year, at the great healing service in the tabernacle, he would be finally healed.

I remember the healing service that year. Buddy couldn't sleep the night before. We were both so excited—I remember being almost out of breath as I pushed him into the tabernacle. At long last, after sixteen years in a wheelchair, Buddy would finally stand, walk, and move about easily.

Finally, the moment came for me to wheel Buddy to the altar, over the straw floor. The preachers, powerful and august men, would lay their hands on him and put oil on his forehead. And as I stood behind Buddy in his chair, he would be healed. It was God's will. We were sure of that.

They applied the oil, they prayed a fervent prayer, loud and long. I peeked because I knew, and he knew, Buddy would stand up for the first time and instead of wheeling him out of the tabernacle, he would run out, jumping and shouting, never to be so physically limited again.

Finally the preacher said, "Amen." I opened my half-opened eyes wide. Everybody did. But Buddy didn't move. His legs were still twisted, his arms still useless. The healing service was over and Buddy was not healed.

I wheeled him out of the tabernacle and back to his room. We sat together in silence for a long time.

At last Buddy spoke. "Earle," he said. "I thought God was going to heal me today. I always believed that in the summer of my sixteenth birthday I would walk at last. I was so sure of it I couldn't wait for today. I knew God could heal me. But He didn't. I believed He wanted me out of this wheelchair, but I was wrong. God wants me to live for Him in my wheelchair and with my crippled body. I will still love Him, and I will still serve Him. I'll not complain about the fact He did not heal me. Instead I'll look for ways to serve Him and others in ways I never could if I had been made whole."

Buddy served the Lord the rest of his life. The nurse who cared for him during one of his hospital experiences, fell in love with him. They were married and had children; two of his sons entered the Christian ministry. He remained a vibrant, positive, powerful voice for God from his wheelchair until the day he died.

Thank God for our great Redeemer who can take our blunders, our failures, even our bad breaks, weave them into a pattern of beauty, and make even our most hurtful disappointments fruitful.

3

OVERWHELMED
BUT HOPEFUL

Modern society's demands leave us overloaded and emotionally drained;
The mind of Christ is the antidote to an overwhelmed spirit.

The room was packed and stifling; even the candles seemed to flicker desperately for lack of oxygen. Andrew glanced about, making out huddled and hunched shadows of friends he'd known for years. They were whispering, mumbling, sobbing—for hours they had been praying for Peter. He was in prison again; this time he was facing certain execution at the hands of bloody Herod.

Andrew shook his head, and he felt a welling of grief from deep within. He couldn't help the thought: *Lord, this is too much.*

First the Lord's new church, growing by leaps and bounds, had been shattered and scattered by the Jewish leadership. Brutally persecuted, thousands fled to the four corners of the earth, leaving only a handful to remain in Jerusalem—a shadow of its former glory.

Then came the internal grappling with the issue of Gentile Christians—Peter led the reform. But dear ones fell away, or remained hurt and embittered. Next came the Antioch incident, with the prophecies from God of impending famine across Rome.

If that weren't enough, now King Herod himself had decided to join the battle. He unjustly arrested many of the disciples' closest friends—some who had followed Jesus from the start. And James, dear James, the Lord's brother. Herod executed him, illegally—by a

Roman centurion's sword, for all the world to see. And the Jewish leadership smirked and applauded, calling for more blood.

"And now Peter—the Rock." Andrew heard his own voice rise above his thoughts, pleadingly, more harsh than he'd intended. And he felt the hand of a nearby sister rest on his shoulder, and squeeze. "It is too much Lord—too much for us to bear."

Several voices around him join in mournful affirmation. "Yes, Lord."

"Lord, please. Do not let them take Peter from us."

"Amen. Yes, Lord."

"Lord, the battle has been long and hard. We are losing. Lord, we are overwhelmed."

I WANT TO GET OFF

Acts 12:24 has an important message that is easily overlooked: "But the word of God continued to increase and spread." It's easy to miss in the context of the chapters preceding this verse, and the one in which the verse is found. They tell about great persecution falling upon the church, of the shadow of Herod covering the earth, of the arrest of Peter, of great opposition by Satan and satanic forces. In the midst of devastation after devastation, springing forth like a rose among the thorns is this embracing word: "But the word of God continued to increase and spread."

We need to give attention to this great verse because it reflects our understandable moods in the face of life. Many people today have a terrible sense of being overwhelmed. We live in a world that every year seems to get more complex, more massive, more unmanageable.

THE TIMES, THEY ARE A-CHANGIN'

Hegel, the philosopher, thought there was no human problem that could not be solved by human beings. He argued that there was no problem that could not be penetrated and encompassed by human thought. That was a long time ago, over one hundred and fifty years ago by the calendar, but more like ten thousand years ago in terms of what has since transpired on the earth and in human affairs. Many people today would chuckle at Hegel's naivety.

Most of us have had that kind of optimism shaken out of us before now by the convulsions of life. It is part of the emotional experience of almost everyone today to feel bewildered and belittled by the overwhelming complexities of life. Rev. Harry Emerson Fosdick quoted this observation, made by a man in his congregation: "I feel like a peanut in Yankee stadium." There are times when we all feel like that—small in the presence of enormity.

We are overwhelmed by change, for one thing. While normal change in life is exhilarating and healthy, too much change, too swiftly, is overwhelming. Things are happening so fast these days we are not able to grasp the facts as they hurry by. At least we cannot grasp the meaning of these speeding facts. Something like an earthquake has shaken the world, shaken down things we once thought to be solid, and swept away old landmarks we once thought permanent. We stand bewildered today in a world of frightening change.

We are also overwhelmed by the expansion of knowledge. We have a deluge of facts breaking upon us before we have an opportunity to assimilate them or know where they are taking us. There are things happening in research laboratories every day that are fantastic beyond belief. With the output of this new data, research periodicals are bulging our libraries. We can be thankful we have computers, because we have developed ways of living too complicated for our brains to process.

This piling up of facts has put an enormous burden on education and new pressures on children and teachers. The average mind is confused and bewildered by it all. How do we find our way through this forest of undigested knowledge?

We are also overwhelmed by the magnitude of our problems. We seem to be up against a new kind of massiveness; everything seems super size, or giant size, or larger. Someone called this, "The age of enormity." Everything is big and getting bigger.

WARS AND RUMORS OF WARS

When everything seems overextended beyond the power of mortals to solve or control, when life confronts us with new questions no one seems to know how to answer, we can't help but ask, what do we do? To whom do we turn?

In international affairs, for example, we face enormous situations that play on all our nerves. War and the threat of war seems always present. *Violence, terrorism, hatred, intolerance*—these are the words most-used today as we face global issues. We make a little progress in one area and find ourselves confronted with mounting difficulties in another. Just when we think one renegade nation is corralled, another breaks out in some innovatively threatening way.

Old animosities, going back through the centuries, break down peacekeeping machinery. Some of these old quarrels seem to be without solution: the Arab versus the Jew; Muslim versus Hindu; democracy versus dictatorship; and now most recently revived, the Muslim versus Christian. The size of these problems is staggering, and all the big decisions must be handled by faulty, finite mortals.

Whether we like it or not, we are all involved in the big decisions and affected by their consequences; but we are not linked with the means of meeting any of them. The late anthropologist Margaret Mead said that we have grown so accustomed to this, so oppressed by the sense that the world has gotten so big and unmanageable that we have accepted the role of nothingness, the helpless feeling that there is nothing we can do that will matter very much. Indeed! *Overwhelmed* is the word.

So, what are we to do when we feel like this? How are we to deal with these dark moods of disheartenment about our own significance? For really, we must not deal with just our problems, but with the mood created by them. We must deal with ourselves in a Christlike way and try to find God's answers.

ANSWERS FOR THE OVERWHELMED

There are at least three Christian answers to the mood created by our feeling of being overwhelmed by life's problems. You will not find these numbered one, two, and three in the Bible, but the general tone and teaching of the Scriptures points to them.

THERE IS GOOD REASON WHY YOU'RE OVERWHELMED

The first thing we must realize, when we are feeling overwhelmed by the magnitude of life, is who God is and who we are—it's theological. Perhaps it will be a bitter pill to swallow, but we must all come to this understanding at last, so we might as well come to it at first: we must all accept the fact of our insufficiency. The fact is, you aren't up to it.

To a point, the mood of being overwhelmed is justified and healthy. We *are* helpless creatures against the forces of the world's turbulent life. Man is not God. This flies in the face of what many self-styled Christians try to preach; in fact, one theologian proudly proclaims that the world has come of age. Modern man is mature; he has learned how to cope with all the important problems without reference to God. So the pinky declares to the brain, "What need have I of you?"

The Bible consistently proclaims the insufficiency of mankind. In fact, God is necessarily the sustainer of all that exists. And yet humans remarkably can presume to believe themselves self-sustaining and independent of God. In truth, we were created to be in relationship with God—our dependence upon Him is essentially our reason for existing.

So the first realistic thing for you to do is to accept your limitations as a creature. Remember, you are not God. Give up your natural inclination to pursue the office of general manager of the universe. And don't worry about it. It's a good thing! You don't have to carry the whole world on your back. Turn it over to all-powerful hands. And remember, the fact that you cannot manage the world does not mean that it is unmanageable or out of control. Fortunately, the affairs of this world are in stronger hands than ours.

This, in part at least, is what faith in God means: trusting in His greatness, in His wisdom, in His power to manage the universe He has made. He has guarded it by some built-in limitations in its structure, beyond which the evils and follies of people cannot go. This is clearly what Jesus meant when He said not to stress even about even the basics of life: "Do not worry . . . your heavenly Father knows that you need them" (Matt. 6:31–32). Paul echoes the Lord in his letter to the Philippians: "The Lord is near. Do not be anxious about anything" (4:5–6). Nothing takes the anxiety out of life quite so much as a consciousness of God's nearness, His greatness, His concern about even the small details of everyday life.

So when you are feeling overwhelmed by life and the problems you are facing, by the questions for which you have no good answers—when you feel "like a peanut in Yankee stadium," settle your mind on this first: accept the fact of your insufficiency. Lighten the load on yourself. Turn it over to stronger hands.

GET BUSY

Another way of dealing with the mood of helplessness in the presence of unmanageable things is to make use of a simple device that is psychologically sound and spiritually essential.

When you get in a low mood about yourself; when you find yourself overwhelmed by a sense of failure or futility; take some small thing, something you can manage, and get it finished. There is wonderful therapy in getting something finished, however small and inconsequential.

If you are a minister or a Christian worker, you are dealing in work that is open-ended. You work with people and ideals. Some days, progress can be measured. Often it cannot. People who work in the area of the mind, in the manipulation of words and ideas, have a curious way of finding relief and rest in physical work—in chopping wood until the back aches or putting a new coat of paint on the porch. The painted porch is something finished. The pile of chopped wood gives a man a sense of getting something useful done. So much of our work, for many of us, is open-ended, unresolved. Often we don't know whether we have finished anything or not.

In past years "westerns" were popular on TV. I used to wonder why they survived all the changes to programming. They speak to a deep mood within us—a longing for something simple. I heard a college professor affirm, "The reason we like westerns is that it is a relief for people living in a complicated world to look—for a while—at a more simple world." Everything is clear in a western: hats are black and white, and something gets settled in the end. Right and wrong are not fuzzy or ambiguous. You can distinguish right away between the good guy and the bad guy. Soon the good guy wins, kisses the pretty girl (or the horse) and rides off triumphantly.

It's not like that in real life. Issues drag on, unresolved: Iraq, Iran, North Korea, China, some new country in Africa, AIDS, addiction. Evil gets punished in a western—the bad guys get shot within the hour. It's all so simple—an escape from the unbearable complexity to a world of satisfying simplicity.

We all want life to be more simple. This is a psychological answer to our feelings of being overwhelmed by life. Turn from the unmanageable to something you can manage. The mother's sage advice is, "When things get too much for me, I go out in the garden and work with my flowers." There is something in the garden that restores her confidence and her focus. She may not be able to manage her children, or a program of the women's society, but she can prune flowers and pull weeds. And she turns for a spell from the big things she can't do to the small things she can. Thus she restores a certain confidence in her own worth.

THINK ON THESE THINGS

The answer that is at the core of your soul's longing is a new attitude—the same mindset as Christ, God the Son. He defines the attitude of the whole New Testament. We as followers of Christ really have an obligation to purposefully move our thoughts over from negative, despairing views of life to life-affirming, hopeful views. And we can do that based on the same set of facts that caused our despair.

Two men looked out of prison bars. The one saw mud, the other stars. The same circumstances, different perspectives. Where are your eyes tending to go in the midst of your difficulties? Are you prone to look to this bleak, hopeless world? Or do your eyes turn to the hope of eternity God promises in His Word?

Even popular Christianity today is prone to draw our eyes to the mud of our own feeble efforts, with pathetic promises that we can accomplish anything for God if we just set our minds (and maybe our backs) to it. We can find ourselves believing the lie that looking toward eternal hope is kind of cheating—as if it were a pie-in-the-sky, impractical faith.

Fundamental to authentic faith is hope that rests in God's sovereign control. Scriptures (Old Testament and New) are constantly affirming that where the mud-fixated vision of the world can only overwhelm, submission to God's control of the future brings hope and peace. Consider a few affirmations of this constant theme, echoed repeatedly throughout the Psalms:

> Be strong and take heart, all you who hope in the LORD (31:24).
>
> We wait in hope for the LORD; he is our help and our shield (33:20).
>
> May your unfailing love rest upon us, O LORD, even as we put our hope in you (33:22).
>
> For you have been my hope, O Sovereign LORD, my confidence since my youth (71:5)
>
> I wait for the LORD, my soul waits, and in his word I put my hope (130:5).

The apostle Paul, in his final exhortation to the Philippian church, similarly challenged believers, but with even more specific (and practical) detail. It's in this same context we saw earlier Paul reminding us that, whatever our anxieties, our Lord is always near (4:5). But Paul goes on in the next two verses to emphasize how to find true freedom from life's cares—turning our eyes from our muddy selves to the heavenly Father:

> Do not be anxious about anything, but in everything, by prayer and petition, with thanksgiving, present your requests to God. And the peace of God, which transcends all understanding, will guard your hearts and your minds in Christ Jesus (4:6–7).

Paul's God-inspired words promise that turning to the heavenly Father with our prayers, petitions, and thanksgiving will bring a peace in our lives that doesn't even make sense. And then he goes into more specific detail about how we can find freedom from overwhelming anxieties. It truly is about our attitude—where we have our vision fixed: "Finally, brothers, whatever is true, whatever is noble, whatever is right, whatever is pure, whatever is lovely, whatever is admirable—if anything is excellent or praiseworthy—think about such things" (v 8).

And what is to be our primary source for such noble and pure thoughts—where can we hope to consistently find our eyes being drawn to the God of all that is right, pure, and good? "Whatever you have learned or received or heard from me, or seen in me—put it into practice. And the God of peace will be with you" (v 9).

God's *Word* (represented by what we've "heard from" Paul) and God's *people* (represented by what we've "seen in" Paul)—these must be our primary sources of inspiration to which we flee, in times of trouble (and in times when life is good). If our attention is fixed on the Father and not the worldly mud, we must listen to His expressed Word, the Bible. And we must also be connected to His body, the church. In these we will be able to fix our minds on what is noble, right, pure, lovely, admirable, excellent, and praiseworthy. Through Christ's Word and His body can we have a godly attitude, come what may. This is how we can think about such things.

You *can* do something about your moods. You can fix your eyes on heaven—upon the assurance that God will one day deliver His people. Christ will return, and our heavenly Father's kingdom will come. It may not be in your power to control the conditions of life, but you have a responsibility to lift up your eyes from these prison bars. This isn't Pollyana stuff—it's the consistent mood of Christ's gospel, rooted in the most bitter human tragedy: Christ's apparent defeat and crucifixion. Yet it is the source of the contagious spirit of resurrection with which the New Testament's pages ring—it's all about true, real-life hope.

E. Stanley Jones, the great preacher-missionary statesman to India, wrote that the early Christians did not say, "Look what the world is coming to." They pointed to the answer and they kept saying, "Look what has come to our world."

"YES, BUT" THINKING

Dr. F. W. Schroder, in an essay titled "Tonic for the Timid,"turned the spotlight on a two-word phrase we often use: "Yes, but." He pointed out the contrast between the way we commonly qualify supposed truths with "Yes, but," and the way the New Testament consistently uses the same syntax, with different meaning.

Against the background of terrific opposition, the early church said, "Yes, but the word of God grew and multiplied." This isn't the world's approach. It is the nature of humanity's mood to concentrate on the negative, to magnify problems, even to discount the good we see and compromise it with a "Yes, but."

Some people bring that despairing mood into the church. The church of Jesus Christ in the world, in our time, is growing, multiplying, and surprisingly vital despite opposition. There are more people in church on any given Sunday in North America than ever before. But instead of rejoicing in that, there are those who express themselves negatively saying, "Yes, but how much genuine Christianity is there really?" Or, "Look at the moral decadence," or, "Think about the outworn structures of the church." On and on they go, page after dreary page of, "Yes, but."

My call to the body of Christ is for a new approach—new to us, but not new to the New Testament. It's an approach modeled by the book of Acts. As we saw earlier, the writer of the book of Acts was talking about great persecution being experienced by the early church, to the point that its existence seemed precarious.

Likewise, read Paul's defiant *Yes, but*: "We are hard pressed on every side, but not crushed; perplexed, but not in despair;

persecuted, but not abandoned; struck down, but not destroyed"
(2 Cor. 4:8–9).

Samuel Rutherford, the great preacher of Anworth, Scotland,
echoed Paul's confidence when he declared to his congregation,
at a time of personal peril and church struggle, "All the windows
of my soul are closed, except the skylight."

SALVATION IS YOURS

Out of the same facts of life you can get despair or hope. Why
not choose not only hope, but the *Source* of true hope? Try on
Christ's attitude—after all, if you're a believer, it's yours for the
taking. We Christians have a moral obligation at this point to
reeducate our moods by redirecting our vision and thoughts; to
strengthen one another by our faith, not to draw others' minds to
the mud with our self-centered "Yes, but" doubts.

I have read a lot of self-styled theologians and intellectuals
coming out with pretty muddy vision—churchmen echoing the
despair of the secular world, mulling over the apparent absence of
God. They speculate that God doesn't live here anymore and
wonder what are we to do? With such an earthly vision, there is
nothing to be done.

When the likes of these and their dark thoughts would crowd
my mind, I read God's words. What a difference the Source
makes. "In this world you will have trouble. But take heart! I have
overcome the world" (John 16:33). We need to saturate our minds
with the uniquely positive, contagious, redeeming words in the
Bible.

Remember the story in the Bible of Shadrach, Meshach, and
Abednego, who were facing the grim prospects of being thrown
into a fiery furnace because of their refusal to bow and worship
an earthly king and proclaim him divine. Their words reach across
the centuries and inspire us today:

We do not need to defend ourselves before you in this matter. If we are thrown into the blazing furnace, the God we serve is able to save us from it, and he will rescue us from your hand, O king. But even if he does not, we want you to know, O king, that we will not serve your gods or worship the image of gold you have set up (Dan. 3:16–18).

We know how the story ended. Their faith and courage were confirmed by the fourth Man in the furnace: God himself, their salvation (and ours).

Wesley still leads us in proclaiming that same victory in his hymn "The Ever-Present Saviour":

> We have through fire and water gone,
> But saw thee on the floods appear.
> We felt thee present in the flame,
> And shouted our Deliverer's Name.

4

OVERCOMING
WORRY

The malady of our time is the multiplication of worry;
To quell worry, find rest and trust in Someone greater.

ot long ago the Heart Association of Chicago invited one hundred top-flight businessmen, the financial magnates of that robust city, to a seminar. They placed before the executives four glass containers. In each container was a human heart, preserved in whatever it is doctors use to preserve things. The first was that of a man who had died in an accident and was exactly as a heart should appear in a middle-aged man. The second was swollen, enlarged to twice its normal size. The doctors explained this was the heart of a hot-tempered, hard-driving business executive who had died in a fit of temper while arguing with a client. The third belonged to a man who had lived under continual tension, refusing to relax or delegate responsibility; he went out one day with a coronary thrombosis. The fourth heart belonged to a man who, in midlife, under the strain of domestic trouble, had suffered a heart attack but had recovered and come back strong to enjoy many years of normal living.

That graphic object lesson by the doctors slowed business in Chicago for almost a week. I hesitate to use this illustration. I don't want anyone here to get such symptoms.

Some people who worry about their hearts shouldn't. None of us should live in fear, and certainly the preacher shouldn't be in the business of increasing anxiety. While this illustration would seem solely a concern for a medical department, it is relevant to the religion department. Let's consider these enemies of human well-being in the light of Christian truth. Let's consider how we should go about taking better care of our hearts.

In the three abnormal hearts, doctors were pointing out three maladies destroying lives in our time: tension, temper, and trouble.

TENSION

Have you heard about the mother of young children who had a nervous breakdown on a Sunday morning in church when the choir was singing the anthem, "Awake, my soul, stretch every nerve"? She had been doing that all week. Everything else in life had been saying that, and she just couldn't take it when the church got to pushing her too.

"Stretch every nerve." While some pressures are essential, it is still an open question whether what we call progress isn't being bought too dearly.

It is doubtful that the Creator designed man for this intense sort of civilization. Our human physique, tough as it is, is not built for the artificial pressures our mechanized society imposes upon us. So much of it is unnatural: artificial noise, artificial speed, artificial stimulation of appetite and desire by advertising media, all ramped up to a higher and higher tempo. Even stomach relief must be fast, fast, fast. How much pressure can the nervous system take?

It reminds me of astronauts who, in preparing for space travel, are put through intense pressures to determine how much heat, cold, speed, confusion, and weightlessness the body can take. Even for those trained and conditioned, the stress is for a limited time. How much stress can you stand and still be able to operate as a human being, under artificial conditions? That's a tough question.

To a lesser degree, condition testing for astronauts is going on in all of us, and we don't know how it's coming out. How much can your spirit take? Where is the breaking point? Humorist James Thurber once quipped that mankind is traveling too fast for a round world and will someday overtake itself.

RELIEF FOR THE ASKING

Three things are sure about these maladies of tension: (1) they are increasing; (2) they are not going to diminish; and (3) each of us has a breaking point. How can we take good care of our bodies and minds when everything, including the church, is demanding us to stretch every nerve? What can we do about these incessant tensions?

There are no easy answers, but there is some helpful advice. It is nothing new, but as C. S. Lewis said, "people need to be reminded more than they need to be instructed."

TRAVEL LIGHT

The first thing is, we must learn to travel light. This means we have to evaluate our "musts." Since there are more things to do than we have energy to accomplish, we have to select; we have to make up our minds about what is supremely important and what is only relatively important. Most of us could go down our lists of activities with God's scale in our hands and weed out 30 percent of the energy-consuming matters that just don't matter.

GO STEP BY STEP

Second, we need to limit our focus. The thing that floors us is the mass attack of problems, the feeling of being swamped. We are seldom bothered by one immediate next step. The stressor is when all the problems, all the confusions, all the decisions attack us simultaneously.

When Jesus said, "Do not worry about tomorrow, for tomorrow will worry about itself. Each day has enough trouble of its own" (Matt. 6:34), He was cautioning about this concern. We cannot bring tomorrow into today and load down the heart with all the burdens of the future.

I often think of a little parable in an old school reader about a clock that suddenly gave up and stopped running. The poor timepiece had figured out how many times it would have to tick in the year (more than 31 million times), and in a panic it quit. But then someone reminded the clock it wouldn't have to tick all of them at once, only one tick at a time.

That old clock helps me to visualize handling my responsibilities. I must not allow myself to think I can accomplish all the ticks—that I can serve all the people or solve all the problems. I have to take it one tick at a time, to focus on the next one. But more so, I can only hope to accomplish each tick by the power of the Maker who wound me up in the first place.

Rather than fooling myself into believing I need to see beyond the next step, I need to simply trust in what God enables me to accomplish. As the old hymn by John Newman beautifully affirms,

> Lead, kindly Light, amid th' encircling gloom, lead Thou
>   me on!
> The night is dark, and I am far from home; lead Thou me
>   on!
> Keep Thou my feet; I do not ask to see
> The distant scene; one step enough for me.

DON'T WORRY

Third, we must learn to relax our souls in God.

There are a lot of books on how to relax—some helpful, others more tiresome than the tension they promise to release. The problem with most is that they promise to bring peace by turning our thoughts inward, calling us to concentrate attention on ourselves. Ironically, the real art of relaxation consists of the opposite: freedom from worry can only be found by becoming selfless. In essence, rather than finding yourself, it amounts to losing the self to God. That was Jesus' solution.

In His Sermon on the Mount, when the Lord challenged His followers to "not worry about tomorrow" (Matt. 6:34), He diagnosed the cause of our worries as our being people "of little faith" (v 30). It's clear from the context of Jesus' teaching here that this kind of faith (so contrary to what the world teaches) is not a faith in ourselves, but rather faith in the one true God, who is outside of and infinitely beyond us. This is the significance of the solution Jesus specifically offers to the problem of worry (and its root, "of little faith"), promised in verse 33: "But seek first his kingdom and his righteousness, and all these things will be given to you as well."

Freedom from worries is never going to be found in that personal kingdom within. True freedom from life's worries is only available to those who have sought, found, and become citizens of Christ's kingdom. Even then, that citizenship is something of which we saved-but-still-fallen human beings must continually be reminding ourselves. (We are prone to lapse back into our default self-governing mode.) It's when we are operating as citizens of Christ's kingdom that He will give "these things" to us. Freedom from worry is not something we find within, but rather it is given to us by God. Nothing fortifies the soul so greatly as when we remind ourselves of this.

Under all our restlessness we find God's strong and everlasting arms. For citizens of His kingdom, it's only a question of whether we will relax ourselves in Him.

TEMPER YOUR TEMPER

This concern is related to the previous one. Often the short fuse of a temper is lit by the smoldering coals of worry. The chronic irritability so characteristic of our time is an emotional pandemic, born partly out of collective fatigue or disharmony of body and mind. Rage is one of the predominant signs of our time. And it's no wonder—for a long time we have been living in emotional crisis, moving from one calamity to another. More than ever, we are a people who need to learn the secret of emotional control.

Jesus cut to the heart of the matter in the very same Sermon on the Mount in which He addressed worrying—the comparison He draws, as recorded in Matthew, strikingly emphasizes the danger of human anger. "You have heard that it was said to the people long ago, 'Do not murder, and anyone who murders will be subject to judgment.' But I tell you that anyone who is angry with his brother will be subject to judgment" (5:21–22). Likewise, James (Jesus' brother) cautioned believers to be "slow to become angry, for man's anger does not bring about the righteous life that God desires" (1:19–20). The book of Proverbs repeatedly characterizes the person who is quick to anger in even more blunt terms: "A fool gives full vent to his anger" (29:11). So how does one avoid the kind of human temper that the Bible calls murderous, folly, and unrighteous?

It's important to understand that, as people created in the image of God—who himself can become righteously angry—our focus should not be upon how to get rid of (or lessen) temper but how to manage it. How can we get it working on the constructive side of life and make it turn the wheels, not just burn out the bearings or blow off the whistle?

Here is how one person did it. He came to the place where he realized he was being defeated in life by his own unruly disposition, and that his disposition was working against him. He was losing friends, his business, and the respect of his employees by his undisciplined temper. He said, "This big factory I own turns out a good product, and people want it and buy it. But the factory that is me—my personal factory—is turning out stuff nobody wants."

The first step is that he realized and acknowledged the problem. Admitting is the first step to repentance. Here are his own words; they are worth pondering:

> Like a little child, I knelt by my bedside and committed my life to the Lord: "Have Thine own way, Lord, have Thine own way. Thou art the potter; I am the clay." I said that. I thought that was the beginning. I would also have to do something myself. I determined I would give as much attention to my personal factory as I did to improving my business. I studied the New Testament and soaked my mind in the Sermon on the Mount. I tried to understand what Jesus meant by "going the second mile" and "turning the other cheek." I tried using the quiet gentleness of His will instead of my own frantic will. I tried to help others and forget myself. I tried to be teachable and willing to learn. I tried to trust God in everything and to get back to my child-heart. At last I came to give the divine gentleness a chance to work through my frenzied nerves. And then I came to the place where I didn't have to try so hard; I had learned what the verse means: "Once it was my trying, His henceforth shall be. Once I tried to use Him, now He uses me."

This is the kind of wisdom that the Bible describes as "fearing the Lord." It is likewise what Paul meant when he challenged Christians to "let this mind be in you, which is also in Christ Jesus" (Phil. 2:4, KJV) and to "be transformed by the renewing of your mind" (Rom. 12:2). It's hard to fathom how drastically, redeemingly, and radically Christ's indwelling Holy Spirit changes us into the likeness of Christ. You, the transformed, will remember what that likeness is when you find yourself provoked to wrath. "When they hurled their insults at him, he did not retaliate" (1 Pet. 2:23, KJV).

TROUBLE

When we talk about trouble, everyone is listening, for we all have a date with it sometime, somewhere, and in some form.

Trouble comes in many forms: somebody blames you for something you did not do; somebody hurts you either deliberately or not; people spread lies about you; another shoves you aside to get ahead; someone close to you loses his or her way morally or ethically; or under your roof there is a critical illness, a financial misfortune, or a bereavement.

Some troubles are so crushing we wonder how any human can take it. We can build machines to lift the strain of weariness off our muscles, but we cannot build anything to lift the strain of trouble from our hearts.

How do you handle trouble? Having someone to face it with you is a help. The "Preacher" of Ecclesiastes put it into perspective:

Two are better than one, because they have a good return for their work: If one falls down, his friend can help him up. But pity the man who falls and has no one to help him up! Also, if two lie down together, they will keep warm. But how can one keep warm alone? Though one may be overpowered, two can defend themselves. A cord of three strands is not quickly broken (4:9–12).

There was a little girl whose mother sent her to the store for a loaf of bread. She was gone a long time, and when she came back her mother asked her what had kept her. She said that a little girl down the street had broken her doll and that she had to help her. He mother asked, "Help her? What could you do?"

She said, "I sat down and helped her cry." That little girl will find a lot to do in life, for troubled people need that—someone to sit down among the broken things with an understanding heart.

This is the sense of God's pronouncement upon creating Adam: "It is not good for the man to be alone" (Gen. 2:18). More than merely not having a mate, God was declaring that human beings—created in His image—are not designed to be alone, even when they have a relationship with their Creator. God made us to be not only in relationship with Him, but with other humans. More so in our fallen state do we need relationships with others. This is why He calls believers to fellowship with His body, the church.

But you do have to go beyond that. When life shakes us down to the depths, our souls need something deeper than human fellowship. That something deeper is what Jesus talked about in the upper room—some*one* to believe in. "Do not let your hearts be troubled," He said. "Trust in God; trust also in me" (John 14:1). The human spirit is tough and can endure profound abuse and still come up unbeaten, provided there is something to believe in, someone who gives meaning to the struggle. Jesus promises that whatever troubles a heart will be resolved by the sole relationship for which we were designed—trusting in the triune God.

A gifted woman lost her son in the Vietnam war. For a while she was bewildered. The minister of her church went to see her, but there was nothing he could say to her that she would listen to. After a while she came to see him, not for help but to tell him how empty she found the high pretensions of religion when the real test came. After all, she said, the church had given her no faith for this sort of thing. Prayer was no good; she had begged God for some kind of answer, and nothing came.

People had told her the usual trite clichés—that time would heal the hurt. And she said, "I don't want that. What these people mean is a sort of anesthetic, and I don't want that. I don't want less awareness. I want more."

Others had told her it would make her a better woman. But she insisted this would be bitter comfort, that her son would be sacrificed so she could be better. No, her son didn't need to die on that account, to make her better.

Still others had tried to help her with the thought that she was not alone in her suffering. After all there were thousands who shared the same trouble. "If I could get comfort out of that," she said, "the suffering of others—I think I would be some kind of monster."

The minister wisely didn't talk back—he just listened and helped her cry. Maybe, she said—maybe she would never find the answer by looking for it; maybe it would have to come, like happiness, on the way to something else. Maybe now she would have to give more of herself, help a little to make a kindlier world. That's what her son died for. And, she added, God's Son too.

Maybe she could do that.

She went out the door with something closer to a smile than she'd had in a long time.

"So," the minister said, "I closed my front door more softly than usual, with the memory of that slight smile, because I knew, even though she didn't yet, that she had found the answer."

The faithful may seek an answer when trouble bears down upon their hearts. Yet they also willingly put their backs under something God wants done. They set their hearts beating with Christ's heart, and they grow steadily and quietly in a faith they are sharing in some measure with the age-long (and ageless) cross. They have become a small but vital and living part of the healing, redeeming purpose of God throughout time.

As the hymnwriter John Greenleaf Whittier (1807–1892) expressed:

> Dear Lord and Father of Mankind,
> Forgive our foolish ways;
> Re-clothe us in our rightful mind,
> In purer lives Thy service find,
> In deeper reverence, praise.
> Drop Thy still dews of quietness,
> Till all our strivings cease;
> Take from our souls the strain and stress,
> And let our ordered lives confess
> The beauty of Thy peace.

5

STILLING
RESTLESSNESS

Restless hearts see meaninglessness and bitterness around them;
Settled hearts look to God for fulfillment of their longings.

Psalm 37 records the words of old King David, a man of experience who is speaking to us: "I was young and now I am old" (v 25). We ought to listen to a man who has lived so long and so successfully. He has something to say, something we need desperately to hear. The tone of this old man's voice speaks of ripened wisdom and the calm of age. His dim eyes have seen and survived much. He has known so many evil people blasted in all their leafy verdure and so many languishing good people revived. His life reflects something of what the poet John Milton penned two millennia later: "Old experience doth attain / To something like prophetic strain" (*Il Penseroso.* Line 173–74).

Life with all its changes has not soured, but rather quieted this man. He does not think of life as an endless maze. Nor does he despise it. He has learned to trust God in it, until life has been cleared of confusion.

What a contrast is this calm, cheerful godliness to the bitter cynicism later found on the lips of his son. To Solomon, old age would bring the burden of melancholy and depression, and with it his summation in Ecclesiastes that "all is vanity." King David's focus was: "Delight yourself in the LORD and he will give you the desires of your heart" (v 4).

Each of us should ask, as early in adulthood as possible, what is life about? We ought to seek a path that will lead us and our families to the fullest life. We ought to discover a path to tranquility in an age of confusion and trouble.

Here are a few clues to that path.

TRANQUILITY

King David was direct when he proclaimed, "Delight yourself in the LORD and he will give you the desires of your heart." Why are so many of us troubled and restless? We suspect it is because of our external circumstances, but the psalmist knew better. The problem is not without, but within.

It is not our changing circumstances but our unregulated desires that rob us of peace. To illustrate, when we are feverish, it is not because of the external temperature, but rather because of the state of our own blood inside. In the same way, it is a mistake to think we would be happy if some trying circumstances were changed. We will not really be happy until we gain release from the wishes that make us unquiet.

How, then, do our desires destroy tranquility? They are our masters, we are at their mercy. Even though we did well when we finally decided in America that slavery was immoral and abolished the slave trade, there is another slavery we have not abolished; a slavery that is very real, very mean, very demanding. It is not the ugliness of the old slave market, or the pain inflicted by the whip upon poor souls pulling at the oars in the hold of a slave ship. Instead, it is the slavery caused by our desires, wants, and wishes.

IDOLS OF DISCONTENTMENT

We tend to make things necessities for our contentment. So whatever thing it is that we place in an elevated position, we make it the lord of our happiness. By our own desires, we give perishable things power over us. We so intertwine our beings with finite and feeble things, that when the blows of life destroy them, our lifeblood fades with them.

It is much like the alpine climber who, bent on reaching the summit of some foreboding height, ties himself to the guide. But when the guide slips, the traveler with him falls to his death. Likewise, the giddy top of fortune's wheel, and the host of travelers who are bent on reaching that artificial summit, tie themselves to their feeble, inanimate gods. And because such things skip by, pass away, and generally disappoint, the silly traveler's pursuits are doomed.

Any person who attempts to build his or her peace on the possession of fleeting joy is sure to be always restless. This is because those who fix their happiness on anything less sufficient than God, will sooner or later experience a time when it will pass from them, or they from it.

Why would one trust his happiness to an unstable vessel? Such a poor, frail craft will inevitably strike on some black rock rising from life's sheer depths, and it will grind itself to powder there. If your life twines around any prop but God, who alone is your strength, it *will* fade away to meaningless, vain vapor.

YOUR HEART'S DESIRE

What shall we do with our slavish wants and desires? "Delight yourself in the Lord." Transfer those desires to Him. Let the affections be fixed and fastened on Him. Make the Lord the end of our longings and the food of our spirits. Is not this the highest form of religious emotion to be able to say, "Whom do I have but God? Possessing Him I desire none beside."

This glad longing after God is the cure for the feverish unrest of desires unfulfilled. Quietness fills the soul that delights in the Lord. Take God as your supreme delight, as your own master attraction, and you shall be freed from the distractions that cause unrest.

Such a soul is still as the great river above the falls when all side currents and dimpling eddies and backwaters are effaced by the attraction that draws every drop in one direction. Or, like the same stream as it nears its end, forgets how it splashed among the rocks of the mountainside and flows now with a calm motion to its rest in the sea. So let the current of your being be set toward God. Then your life will be filled and calmed.

What is the result of delighting in God or bringing our desires to Him? Fruition: "He shall give you the desires of your heart." At this point we must be careful not to apply some vulgar interpretation to this great promise by making it mean something it does not mean. There is a prosperity gospel, which is not the gospel, that states that all will be good for those who delight in the Lord; that God will give all earthly blessings wished for. In truth, sometimes we will get them; sometimes we will not. The psalmist intends to take us to a deeper meaning than that.

God is the heart's desire of those who delight in Him. The promise is that the people who wait on the Lord and delight in Him will have Him, their heart's desire. As sunshine flows into the opened eye and breath of life into the expanding lung, so the fullness of God fills the waiting, wishing soul. To delight in God is to possess that delight. In Psalm 24 David describes a "generation of those who seek him, who seek your face, O God of Jacob" (v 6). He calls upon them to "lift up your heads, O you gates; be lifted up, you ancient doors, that the King of glory may come in (v 7).

The desire after God brings peace by putting all other wishes in their place. The counsel here does not enjoin the extinction of desire. Rather it subordinates other needs and appetites to the longing for God. This is consistent with Jesus' call to all disciples: "But seek first his kingdom and his righteousness, and all these things will be given to you as well." (Matt. 6:33). Let that be your dominant desire—the one that controls and underlies all the rest.

Seek God in everything. Only then will you be able to bridle the cravings that would otherwise tear your heart.

When the sun leaps in the heavens, the stars that were so bold all night hide. Yet they are still there. The more we set our affections on God, the more we shall enjoy because we subordinate His gifts, and the less we shall dread their loss. If you have God for your enduring substance, you can face all conditions calmly, saying: "Give what Thou canst; without Thee I am poor, and with Thee rich. Take what Thou wilt away."

There is a way to tranquility and it is, in part, to still our eager desires; to arm ourselves against feverish hopes, shivering fears, and certain disappointments by making sure we delight ourselves in the Lord, knowing He shall rest those desires in and with himself.

PATH OF FREEDOM

Included in David's promise that those who delight in the Lord will have their heart's desire, is the call to "Commit your way to the LORD; trust in him and he will do this" (Ps. 37:5). Literally David is saying, "Roll your path on God; leave to Him the guidance of your life, and you shall be at peace on the road."

I do not take this to mean that we are to apply this grand truth only to momentous decisions. It concerns all the paths of life's road. At times the road will come to a watershed, and a person's future may depend on choosing to turn right or left. That person needs guidance then, and he or she knows it. But the need is no less in the small, hourly decisions, because our lives are made up of a series of trifles, and each involves a separate act of the will.

IN THE DETAILS

Character is made much the same way as coral reefs are built: by a multitude of tiny things that united can withstand a mighty ocean. Consider how the greatest events in our lives grow out of the smallest. Likewise, practiced habits have the power to make any little action of the mind almost instinctive.

It is of far more importance that we should become accustomed to applying this precept of seeking guidance from God to the trifles of our daily existence, than even to the momentous decisions that come our way. If we have not learned the habit of committing the daily monotonous steps to Him, we shall find it hard to seek God's help when we come to a fork in the road.

THE TRUE GUIDE

How shall we then live a tranquil life? Leave the perplexity of choosing life's path to God. Here again, subordination does not mean extinction. This does not mean that we do not have wishes and a will for our own life. Our own wishes for ourselves are always an element in our choice. But they must be secondary and not primary. Our first question should not be, what would I like? Rather, what does God will? We do not lose our will. The will is always the master of our passions, desires, whims, and habits. But the will is to be servant of God. The will should silence the cries of desire, and itself be silenced that God may be heard.

Our will is like Moses of old. You will remember he stood as the lawgiver captain at the head of the army, ready to march. He, however, would not advance until he saw the pillar lift from above the sanctuary in the desert showing the way.

Our wills do not die, they become subordinate to God's will. The will is a strong leader; it can lead through a whole body of passions and desires, but that will ought to be taught not to move, not to make a decision, until we discover which way the pillar is going for us. We discover this by committing our way to the Lord, not unto duty or conscience, but unto God.

It is important that we submit our judgment to God in the confidence that His wisdom will guide us. I do not think this is an encouragement to laziness. Nor is it admonishing us to follow our first impulse. Rather, because we commit our way to the Lord, we seek diligently and prayerfully that we might know the will of God. God counsels people who will use their own minds to discover what His counsel is. Let the eye be fixed on Him, and He will guide. If we chiefly desire and with patient impartiality try to be directed by Him, we shall not want for direction from Him.

All of this is possible because we delight in the Lord. We need to still our own desires if we would know God's direction, and nothing else stills our desires as does delighting in Him. To delight in Him is the condition of all wise judgment.

Do not neglect the keys of tranquility for your life: joy in God and trust in His guidance. These open for us the doors of the quiet way of the Most High, where all the roar of the busy world dies upon the ear and the still, small voice of God deepens the silence and hushes the heart.

Be quiet, and you will hear God speak; delight in God, and you will be quiet!

6

CONQUERING FEAR

Fears grip and debilitate;
Jesus offers mastery through His perfect love.

One Thursday morning the newspaper carried the picture of Mrs. Mary Demske of St. Petersburg, Florida. A police officer was trying to tell her it was safe to return to her home. Neighbors flushed two would-be thieves from her residence. Mrs. Demske was 100 years old, her face deeply lined, her eyes dimmed by the years. But you could see it there, written unmistakably on her face: hers was the picture of fear.

Fear has no respect for age. We all know something about it.

During His life on earth, Jesus continually confronted the fear problem. He used the words *fear, anxious, troubled,* and *afraid* often. "Fear not," "Do not be anxious," "Let not your heart be troubled, neither let it be afraid." And with good reason—often He met people who were afraid. Often He encountered fear in the lives of those He loved, people who believed in Him.

Basil King wrote a book titled, *The Conquest of Fear.* He prefaced the book with these words:

When I say that during most of my life I have been the prey of fear I take it that I am expressing the case of most people. I cannot remember a time when a dread of one kind or another was not in the air. In childhood it was the fear of going to bed. Later it was the fear of school. Later still, the experience in the morning waking with the feeling of dismay at the amount of work to be done before night. In one form or another fear dogs every one of us; the mother is afraid for her children; that father is afraid for his business; the clerk is afraid for his job; hardly a man is not afraid that some man will do her or him a bad turn; hardly a woman is not afraid that what she craves may be denied her or that which she loves may be snatched away. I am ready to guess that all the miseries wrought by sin and sickness put together would not equal those we bring on by the means which perhaps we do the least to counteract.

You probably do not agree with Basil King's conclusion of the book, as I did not. It is more Buddhist than Christian, but I think we can agree with his premise that fear is a major problem.

As Christians, we are to face every problem in God's grace. To do that we are going to have to take a different starting point than most books on fear take. Many such books can be notoriously negative and inevitably unsatisfying because they start from the false premise that fear is an enemy, an evil and harmful emotion to be driven out. You will not win the battle with fear if you start there. One can never come out right from a false start.

THANK GOD FOR FEAR

Fear is an elemental emotion, part of your native equipment. It is God-given and, like any other normal emotion, has a constructive purpose in this fallen world. Our real problem is not how to get rid of fear but how to respond to it.

The animals are aware of fear's purpose. There is no animal without fear. The shallow theology that teaches that fear is abnormal has not yet reached the chipmunk. He has never read the "fear" books. That is why he is still alive and chattering.

For some creatures like the deer and rabbit, fear is the sole weapon of defense. It is not an enemy at all but an ally. Startle a rabbit in a thicket and what happens? The sense of impending danger starts a nervous reaction which, quicker than you can say "rabbit," shoots a powerful stimulant from his glands into his running apparatus and he is gone with the wind—gone with a speed he could not manage without the stimulus of fear. Any deer that cannot leap ten feet out of an afternoon nap and come down with his legs pounding is not liable to last long in a forest of wildcats or hunters.

We have some of that same equipment in our bodies, but with us, it is linked with more than glands and legs. It is tied in with our thinking machinery and our complex emotional machinery—it's integrated into our souls. This is why human fear is immensely complicated and why we must be more realistic in our understanding of its function. For created-in-the-image-of-God animals, it's a spiritual matter. Those books on getting rid of fear do not reach the spiritual depths of the problem.

The fact is, we are not wise to rid ourselves of all fear. I need my children to have a healthy fear of some things. There are too many reckless drivers, too many evil people, too many wild animals for me to afford the luxury of naively whistling in the dark. At our house we wanted our children (and now our grandchildren) to be afraid of playing with matches, razor blades, or bottles marked "poison."

Not all our fears are groundless or wasted. The worst of them are rooted in a fallen, sinful reality, that no amount of self-deception can (nor should) drive out. For instance, we are not yet ready to dispense with fear in the building of society. We are not yet ready to scrap the police department or courts of law. We have to go on making and enforcing laws to strike dread in the hearts of people who have no inclination to do right for right's sake and may be deterred from menacing society only by a healthy fear of consequences.

FEARS THAT CONTROL

Nevertheless, fear is a high-voltage emotion. When fear overshoots the mark or overleaps the boundaries, it becomes a destructive, disintegrating force. Phobias can be fatal.

It is an interesting exercise to count all the phobias listed in the dictionary. Their name is legion, and they are all bad: acrophobia, fear of height; claustrophobia, fear of closed places; agoraphobia, fear of open places; neophobia, fear of the new; pathophobia, fear of disease; photophobia, fear of lights; spermaphobia, fear of germs; ergophobia, fear of work; (okay, that last one is not in the dictionary; but I think it should be).

More than seventy-five phobias are listed all the way from ereuthophobia, the fear of blushing (perhaps we could do with a little more of that one) to phobophobia, fear of all things. These are abnormal, irrational fears; not funny, but tragic. Monstrous evil comes out of misused fear, fear that exceeds what's healthy, taking control of us. And they all illustrate and underscore my premise, that the problem we face is not how to get rid of fear, but how to respond to fear as God intended for us.

God designed in us a natural "fight or flight" reaction to circumstances that pose a threat so we might preserve our lives, or the lives of others. Fear in this sense is our natural, God-given instinct and reflex.

Often children take delight in causing another person to flinch when they swing or act as if they're going to hit another in the face. "Made you blink," they'll boast. But of course, the blinker is reacting with good reflexes and instincts—he's healthy, responding the way God designed him to protect his eyes. The one who doesn't blink when threatened is the one who should be concerned.

SPURS TO KNOWLEDGE

Fear can be a spur to knowledge. Ironically, it is the thing we probably most fear—the unknown—that drives us to explore. From our earliest days there is the fear of shapeless shadows of supposed evil that lurk in the darkness of ignorance. The torment of that fear has been the motivation to pursue knowledge in so many areas that we are tempted to say, "Thank God for the fears that stimulate thought; thank God for the fear of disease that has driven people to work in laboratories hunting for cures and causes; thank God for the fear of want and hunger that has prodded us to invention and conservation." That is what fear is for: it is a prod to the emotions, a torment in the soul to drive us out of darkness into light.

SHINING LIGHT ON MONSTERS

There's an old story about the science teacher in a boys' school who had an uncanny knowledge of animal life. You could show him the bone of any animal, and he could name the animal. Give him the scale of a fish, and he could identify the fish and tell you its native waters and the season of its spawning. That was his world.

One day the boys attempted to play a trick on the old man. They got the skeleton of a bear, stuffed it with cotton, sewed over it a skin of a lion, fastened on its head the horns of a Texas steer, and on its feet they glued the hoofs of a wild buffalo. They spent many nights on the trick and did a good job constructing their grotesque beast.

One afternoon when the professor was taking his post-lunch nap they opened the door to his study, tiptoed in, and set up their monstrosity. Behind the door they gave out an unearthly growl such as never before was heard on land or sea. The professor stirred himself, tumbled off his cot, and stood upright, reacting with enough fear to justify the experiment. Then, through their peepholes, the boys witnessed a surprising transition. The old man rubbed his eyes again, looked at the fierce teeth, the horns, and finally the split hoofs. He said, "Thank God it's herbivorous, not carnivorous," and went back to finish his nap. His knowledge had calmed him. He knew any animal with horns and split hoofs was a vegetarian, preferring grass to a professor.

For centuries people were terrified by the sun's eclipse; even today, in some lands unenlightened by scientific knowledge, many still become hysterical at that weird spectacle. But you and I are not afraid of an eclipse; we know what it is. Our knowledge has allayed the fear.

Why do we fear the dark? Because we do not know what is in it; we do not understand its sounds and shadows. In Shakespeare's *A Midsummer Night's Dream*, Theseus cautions, "Or in the night, imagining some fear, / How easy is a bush suppos'd a bear!" (V.1.23–24). We are not afraid in a broad daylight, for then we can see the bush is a bush. Light makes the difference.

CASTING OUT FEAR

As healthy (health preserving) and motivational as fear can be, there nevertheless is a type of fear that is not God's design or will for our lives.[1] In fact, this kind of fear is antithetical to His nature. This is the consuming fear that masters us or even enslaves us. Instead of the "fear of the Lord" that Proverbs describes as being the beginning of wisdom, we find ourselves fearing the idols we've constructed in our lives and all the threats they wield over our heads.

When fear of unemployment shifts from motivation to a self-constructed scheme that would substitute reliance upon God, then we are living in fear *of an idol,* not *of the Lord.* And when fear of failure so consumes us that we become workaholics, we find ourselves with our eyes fixed on the idol of success, rather than on Jesus. Or when we drown out our pain with some form of drunkenness or addiction, we are bowing to the mind-numbing idol of denial, rather than relying upon the filling and healing of God's Holy Spirit.

To "fear the Lord" is to be in right relationship with God—one of loving reliance, in which we know our Creator for who He is, and respect and give Him due awe for the infinite attributes that comprise His being. Fear of the Lord appreciates that this is the Creator of the universe who loves and reveres you. The depth and breadth of our relationship to Him is awesome. Actually, it's better described as ineffable.

DRIVING OUT THE FEAR

This is why John can state emphatically, "There is no fear in love. But perfect love drives out fear." And then he presses the point even further: "The one who fears is not made perfect in love" (1 John 4:18).

There is one antidote to destructive fear that would enslave and rule us—one means of toppling the idol that presumes to demand our homage. It's what John describes as "living in love," or more to the point, living in God. They are one and the same, because God himself "is love" (v 16). This love relationship with God has nothing to do with dreading the threat of some big stick He's supposedly wielding, "because fear has to do with punishment" (v 18). God's brand of love (the only true love) is free of fear and free of threat. It's perfect.

There is a beautiful irony in this truth: the one who fears the Lord has nothing else to fear. That's because a God-fearer knows where his or her true reliance rests—in God's love (v 16).

So, who are these God-fearers? They're all those who have acknowledged Jesus is the Son of God and have God's Holy Spirit living in them (v 15). It's that simple. We all need some reminding from time to time. It's too easy for us to forget the truth we know deep in our souls—that God has "given us of his Spirit" (v 13).

Predictably, that's when we tend to find ourselves struggling with debilitating fears. In fact, we could sum up that whenever controlling fears raise their heads in our lives, we should look at them as symptoms of a deeper problem: our love for God is not so "perfect."

Remember, perfect love will have none of it. After all, when you grasp (and truly believe) the amazing truth that God actually loves you—perfectly, then what idol of fear could ever rule you?

Cling to it when darkness threatens—when those bushes in the shadows are starting to look a lot like bears. You know the Truth—you know Him in person.

7

COMFORTING
TROUBLE

In this world we will always have trouble; Jesus said as much.
God's gift of a Counselor is the ultimate comfort in troubling times.

In an English class, I was told that in the construction of a sentence one should not use the same word over and over. I wished in those days my teacher knew more about the Bible, particularly the writings of Paul. Paul was governed by a higher law when he wrote. Time and again his sentences seem to just run away.

Often he uses the same word over and over again—but not because of a deficient vocabulary. His repetition is deliberate. "Here is a fact that is impossible to overemphasize," he seems to be saying. Indeed, here is something that can stand up to the colossal strain of life and the fierce severity of death. So it is, in the doxology that opens 2 Corinthians Paul takes the word *comfort* and rings it out five times.

This is experience; this is autobiography. The great apostle is not spinning airy theories nor weaving pleasant fantasies. He is not narrating events from a detached vantage point; he is living these words. Who would be interested in hearing a person philosophize about facing troubles who has never experienced any?

Yet much of our religion is precisely that: looking at a map, not living in the land. Paul is different. He has been there; he is there; he knows from experience what he is talking about. The words he penned to the Christians at Corinth are direct from his heart.

Paul had a right to speak on this theme. His was not a sheltered life. He knew stoning and shipwreck, flogging and imprisonment, ill health and opposition, the misunderstanding of friends and the diabolical devices of foes. His was a life of discomfort. We can trust what he has to say about how Christians face trouble.

TAKE COMFORT

What does Paul mean by *comfort*? Not what we often mean. The person on the street talks about a comfortable income, home, church. The word *comfort* has been weakened, cheapened, and sentimentalized so much that it stigmatizes religion as sentimental escapism. Please do not think of Christian comfort as something weak. Do not blur moral issues and turn religion into a cushion against the hard facts of life. Christian comfort must never camouflage the cross or superficially use consolatory phrases to hypnotize the troubled mind into a condition of torpid tranquility. Too often the comfort defined by the world is a kind of spiritual anesthetic; the peace of God as a tranquilizer.

Paul has something different in mind. His word for *comfort* is one of the most powerful in the New Testament. *Paraklesis* (comfort) means "calling in to help." It is the summons that brings reinforcements to one's aid. The Bible speaks of the Holy Spirit as the "Comforter," a designation from the same root word. The corresponding word in Latin is *Advocate*, the counsel for the defense. So when the Bible speaks of the Holy Spirit as the "Paraclete" or "Comforter," it does not just mean Counselor. It is closer to the Reinforcer; Strengthener; the Giver of power, might, and victory. Our English word *comfort* originally meant the same thing. Here then is the important distinguishing characteristic about Christian comfort. Paul's teaching is that we can have our total personality supernaturally reinforced. There is nothing weak or sentimental about that.

We are not to be equipped with blinders until we cannot see the disquieting facts of life. We are rather to be armed with the whole armor of God to make us adequate for life as it really is. Christian comfort faces trouble by replenishing our spent resources, working a spiritual renovation, flooding the entire being with radiance and resilience. Here is a comfort strong with the omnipotence of God himself.

From this wellspring Paul could draw and proclaim, "Praise be to the God and Father of our Lord Jesus Christ, the Father of compassion and the God of all comfort" (2 Cor. 1:3). He learned what we all need to learn: Only the measureless mercy of heaven could avail adequately for the multiple miseries of earth. We are dependent on "the God of all comfort."

COLD COMFORTS

But we are experts at trying other sources for comfort in our troubles. Perhaps you are looking to other sources at this moment.

Some people look for comfort in science and technology, as though a day would come when all life's frictions, stresses, and frustrations would be charmed away by miraculous inventions of a scientifically awakened world. Those hopes and promises were being declared over a century ago, and the fulfillment is long overdue, confirming that our best efforts are actually a vain hope.

Others have gone seeking comfort in nature. It is understandable, because there is a sort of strengthening for the soul in the stillness of the mountains and valleys, lakes, and oceans. The problem with nature is it tends to fool us, because often nature merely reflects the mood we bring to it. Nature gives back the joy or sorrow through which we view it. Sometimes, therefore, natural beauty can hurt rather than heal the soul.

Others turn to psychological suggestion. Phrases such as, "Every day and in every way I am getting better and better," seem to promise a lift to individual life and society. The point is, if you can say such words often enough, and with enough confidence, you will achieve (so we are told) a satisfactory readjustment to your mood, if not to your life. This is psychology's scheme of working out our own salvation. But about that utopian optimism we need only say: It is too naive and shallow to be true.

There are brave souls with the temperament that leads them to look for comfort amidst the troubles of life in the practice of a stoic philosophy. There can seem to be nobility there. Resolutely, the stoic sets himself to be the master of his fate, the captain of his soul, and even the architect of his destiny. Self-control, self-sufficiency, self-determination—these are the stoic's watchwords. "Soul," he may say, "play the man. Don't surrender to your emotions, don't give in to weakness. Your will is unconquerable; crush down feelings; defy fate."

While it might have a nostalgic romanticism about it, it cannot help but amount to a vanity of vanities. Such a philosophy is another form of denial, perhaps with the variation of self-deification and aggrandizement. It plays to that old temptation posed by the serpent to Adam and Eve—you can be your own gods.

Still others, and their number is legion, go to the opposite extreme and seek comfort in a hedonistic ethic: "Let us eat, drink, and be merry, for tomorrow we die." This is attractive to a pleasure-seeking world wanting to throw off the restraints of religion. The word of the hedonist is, "Let us not worry about rights and wrongs, taboos and conventions. The secret of a comfortable existence is the ability to relax." In fact, that word *relax* is used often today to invite people to drift into materialism and self-absorption. The creed of the hedonist offers the fleeting image of contentment. As Mick Jagger intoned when hedonism was coming of age, they still just "can't get no satisfaction."

THE MIGHTY GRASP

So we come to the great apostle and his discovery: "Praise be to the Father of compassion and the God of all comfort." There was a time when Paul tried to find comfort for his troubles in pride of nationality, in righteousness of life, in blamelessness of conscience. But the more he tried, the more desperately uncomfortable he became. When he met Christ Jesus and tasted something of the Lord's Spirit, that day of comfort and peace of God entered him and possessed him. It became so real and pervasive that never from that moment were the thousand vicissitudes of his life able to dislodge it.

> Let me no more my comfort draw
> From my frail hold on Thee;
> In this alone rejoice with awe,
> Thy mighty grasp of me.[1]

This is what the revelation of God in Christ has given us: the certainty of a divine hand upon our lives, the assurance of God's "mighty grasp of me." There is for us the healing power of the dimensions of eternity, the resurrection music of the promise, *I will not leave you comfortless; I will come to you.* This is not dead dogma, it is life-transforming truth; truth which can be verified by anyone today. This is the comfort of the Lord.

THE BREADTH OF COMFORT

"Praise be to the God and Father of our Lord Jesus Christ . . . who comforts us in all our troubles" (2 Cor. 1:3–4). What a great word for everyone reading this: "in all our troubles." There is no conceivable situation to which this does not apply. No one knew that better than did the apostle Paul, for he had tested it thoroughly.

There are four species of trouble to which human beings are heir.

PHYSICAL TROUBLE

Paul knew something about this because he was a man who had a "thorn in [his] flesh" (2 Cor. 12:7); that is, his recurring, frustrating bouts with what probably was some crippling illness. We know of many other troubles were inflicted upon him. Imagine suffering indescribable squalor in a first-century jail. Paul was stoned by mobs, not to mention flogged by the lashes of the Roman police. He suffered so much physically that, in his letter to the Christian Galatians, he affirmed, "I bear on my body the marks of Jesus" (6:17). But through all this he declared that he found the grace of God sufficient for him. In fact, so much so, that at midnight in the dungeon at Philippi he and Silas could sing loudly and triumphantly for joy.

MENTAL TROUBLE

Even more torturous at times is the anxiety that can come upon us. Paul knew the anxious care of being an ancestor in the faith to many people. He bore the worry of seeing young churches corrupted into heresy and young converts relapsing into paganism. He was weighted with the future of the work. But through this he found the peace of God would stand sentinel over heart and mind.

The great challenge for many of us today is the struggle of the mind to bear up under the weight of the emotional and mental strains life puts on us. The concern of family, health, financial security, world distress, and a host of other conditions visit us with increasing frequency. There is in God comfort for all our mental troubles.

SPIRITUAL TROUBLE

It is not wise to idealize the great apostle. Paul had been a blasphemer and a persecutor, "breathing out murderous threats against the Lord's disciples" (Acts 9:1). If in the moment when he fell from his horse at the Damascus gate he had broken his neck or had been trampled to death, it would have been no more than he deserved.

He knew that, for he unequivocally declared in his first letter to Timothy, "I was shown mercy so that in me, *the worst of sinners*, Christ Jesus might display his unlimited patience as an example for those who would believe on him and receive eternal life" (1:16, emphasis added). This was no false humility on Paul's part—he was a notorious and zealous persecutor of God's people. He hated Christians because of their faith, so he intended no hyperbole when he described himself in his former state as "the worst" kind of sinner.

But then the miracle of everlasting mercy of Christ met him, and sent him to serve with the passionate gratitude of the forgiven. What is the guilt you carry? What are the past sins that weigh on your soul in the dark night of regret? Whatever, these are comforting words for you: in Christ Jesus there is mercy and unlimited patience; there is forgiveness, full and complete. God indeed comforts us in all our moral and spiritual troubles.

THE LAST GREAT, FINAL TROUBLE—DEATH

The greatest source of trouble is the last one, the sting of death, the menace of the king of terrors. The ancient civilizations of Greece and Rome were haunted by the grim, inexorable shadow of mortality. The last enemy that would be destroyed was death.

"But thanks be to God!" Paul would exclaim, "He gives us the victory through our Lord Jesus Christ" (1 Cor. 15:57). Sin and death are conquered through Jesus' work on the cross, so that with Paul we can defiantly proclaim, "Where, O death, is your victory? Where, O death, is your sting?" (v 55).

As years pass and health fails, we face the fear of the unknown. What a comfort to know Him who lives beyond death and the grave and is able to comfort us in the last, darkest trouble of all.

WHAT TROUBLES YOU?

So then there is no situation to which God's comfort does not apply. This is the absolute range of the Lord's comfort. Now it is important for you to put your experience into this great truth. What is the trouble you face?

If it is physical, the word of the Lord for you is that your physical life, every atom and every breath, is in the hands of the One who knows and cares and understands. Since He was afflicted with all the afflictions we can face, He is infinitely resourceful to make us more than conquerors.

Is it the mental burden of anxiety that now troubles you? The door is open to you to cast your burdens on the Lord—to say to Him every morning and every evening, "Father, into Your hands I commit my spirit, knowing that You will accept responsibility for me, since I trust in You."

Is it moral or spiritual struggles that trouble you? Then seek to believe the central affirmation of your faith that there is no limit to His love: "He breaks the power of cancelled sin, He sets the prisoner free."

Is it the shadow of mortality that robs you of your peace? The Christ of the resurrection is at hand to tell you that what looks like the closing of a door and the putting out of a light is, in fact, the opening of the most wonderful gateway and the sunburst of the most inexpressible glory. There is no malady to which this divine therapy does not apply. "Praise be to the Father of compassion and the God of all comfort."

COMFORT AND OTHERS

But Paul's description of the "God of all comfort" in his second letter to the Corinthians isn't just about you. God "comforts us in all our troubles, so that we can comfort those in any trouble with the comfort we ourselves have received from God" (1:4).

This is an important aspect in the process by which God helps us triumph over our troubles. True religion is never self-centered and introverted; it never clutches the comforts of God to its own need. Whenever I treat the gospel as a prescription to help me relax or secure me against what is difficult and disagreeable, it becomes a caricature of Christ's teaching. The purpose of being comforted by God is that you should go out and mediate the same gift to other struggling souls.

The whole mystery of suffering is illuminated here. The reason for the rough places in life is that we may, through the difficult experiences, become agents of God's help to others. It is God's intention that our suffering be transmuted into love. Thornton Wilder caught this truth and declared, "In love's service only the wounded soldiers can serve."

Ironically, God used Paul's tormenting handicap, his thorn in the flesh and his experience of God's sufficient grace, to give him the power he might otherwise never have possessed to reach and to touch other lives. Typically the real healers whom God uses in this ailing world are those whose peace has been bought with a great price. This is part of the redeeming efficacy of the cross. Christ suffered there and is now the Savior for a suffering world. To comfort others, this is the obligation imposed upon us who have been ourselves comforted by God.

It is awful to worry about self, our security, our success in this tormented world of refugees and disinherited people, with two thirds of the world's population either undernourished or starving. It is an awful thing for any church to be centered upon self, its status, its prestige, its venerable traditions, when the burden of Christ's message is that the kingdom of God is greater than any church, and the church that persists in seeking its own life will certainly lose it in the end.

It is pathetically easy for self to work its way even into the heart of religious life. But Jesus said, "If anyone would come after

me, he must deny himself and take up his cross and follow me"
(Mark 8:34).

> O strengthen me that while I stand
> Firm on the rock and strong in Thee,
> I may stretch out a loving hand
> To wrestlers with the troubled sea.[2]

Where is Christ to be found today—the real presence of
Christ? Obviously, in Word, sacraments, and worship, but also in
the flesh and blood of every needy person. Did not Christ say,
"For I was hungry and you gave me something to eat, I was thirsty
and you gave me something to drink, I was a stranger and you
invited me in" (Matt. 25:35); and with that, His explicit warning,
"Whatever you did for one of the least of these brothers of mine,
you did for me" (v 40).

Here is the presence of Christ—in the troublesome neighbor;
in the handicapped sufferer; in the poor bungler who has made a
mess of his life; in the woman who carries a great tragedy in her
heart; in the jaded youth who will tell you he has no use for religion or God. This is where you will find Christ, "in the least of
these." If we are not prepared to serve Christ at these points of
need, all our expressions of love to God are worthless, and our
religious professions are frivolous.

The question for us all is, can we face the challenge? The burden
of the world's great need could break us down. The yoke of the
world's callousness could crush us, except for the fact that Christ
carried this burden and bore this yoke.

So it is not ourselves, it is Christ in us who offers the incredible glory of calling ourselves Christians. It is Christ moving
through us out into the lives of others, who strengthens and rein-
forces them through us. That's the answer to all life's troubles.

8

PERSEVERING
THROUGH AFFLICTION

Evil holds power over this fallen world;
We need fear no evil for God is with us.

One day a fire broke out in Thomas Edison's laboratory, burned it completely, and destroyed many valuable but unfinished experiments. Later, walking through the water-drenched wreckage, he found a little package of papers tied neatly and tightly together with a string. The package was soaked and fire-scarred, but by some freak of chance had been left intact. Mr. Edison opened it and at the center of the package was a photograph, a picture of himself, scorched around the edges but still undamaged. He looked at it for a moment, then picked up a piece of charcoal from the floor and wrote across the face of the picture, "It didn't touch me."

It is not possible to live life without troubles coming in various ways and with some degree of regularity. With trouble comes reason for anxiety. Is it possible to be able to say of those troubles, "They didn't touch what is deepest within"?

There is no wall high enough to shut out trouble. The fire still burns the edges. There is no life, however pure, that is immune from it. There is no trick, however clever, by which we can evade it—not by escapism, not by fantasy, not by denial of reality, not by drugs or alcohol or happy pills, not even by miraculous intervention can we get beyond the reach of trouble. Trouble is universal and impartial. Jesus himself got into it.

WHY ME?

People who do not believe this often utter the petulant prayer, "Why? Why should this happen to me? What have I done to deserve this?" Interestingly it is heard even in some thankful prayers people use to express their gratitude for deliverance. They seem to suggest that by some merit in themselves they were spared the evils that came upon others.

After the San Francisco earthquake, which was followed by fire that reduced the city to shambles, a newspaper reporter noticed a liquor distillery standing intact in the midst of the devastation, and he wrote:

> If, as they say, God spanked this town
> For being over-frisky,
> Why did he burn the churches down
> And spare Old Hopalong's whiskey?

No, that theology will not stand up—not the kind of thinking that would demand God protect the righteous from trouble and visit disasters only upon evil people. History has repeated itself. I was told that in Los Angeles the buildings that suffered most from the great earthquake there were the churches.

FEAR NO EVIL

There must be another sense in which we get beyond the reach of trouble. I am reminded that the psalmist David made an interesting statement in the Twenty-third Psalm when he said, "I will fear no evil" (v 4). In other words, evil may come—will certainly come—but it will not destroy me or paralyze me.

Why? Because "you [God] are with me." There is then this high sense in which David was beyond the reach of his troubles. We need to feel the force of that. There is a place of divine-human relationship where we can come to the point, in our faith, that trouble does not damage us—it certainly cannot destroy us. In this place, we can be free from anxiety.

Journey with me along this road. Let us see if there are some points in our lives where we can apply this suggestion. To do that we will need to attempt to classify our troubles.

MANAGEABLE ANXIETIES

Beginning at the lowest and simplest level, some of our troubles are reasonably manageable. I mean, some of the evils that befall us have power to harm only or mainly through our fear of them. They are not, in themselves, that formidable. We get beyond their power when we get beyond the anxiety.

Lloyds of London, probably the most famous insurance company, has made millions of dollars out of fear, betting with people that the disaster they anticipate will never happen. Think of all the bridges we cross before we reach them, all the shadows we cast, all the ghosts we conjure up. This is a malady that afflicts us all. We are afraid of so many things that in themselves have no power to hurt us except through the torment of the anxiety they inspire.

Obviously we should not underestimate real dangers, nor, as we saw in the previous chapter, join the chorus of those who despise fear as wholly evil. Remember, fear is a useful, indispensable element in preservation, a divinely implanted emotion for our protection.

But then there is anxiety—insidious, gnawing away at our spirits. Where fear can preserve life, anxiety drains it away. One of our great needs is to keep anxieties manageable. One of the great contributions faith makes to wholesome life is at that very point. Nothing takes anxiety out of life so much as an awareness deep within of God's nearness and His loving concern for us.

"I will fear no evil, for you are with me." The anxiety David speaks about is the common one of death. The psalmist likens it to a shadow: "Even though I walk through the valley of the shadow of death." When life is undergirded by a consciousness of God's presence and concern we are released from the anxiety of many shadows and get beyond the reach of many evils.

TURNING ANXIETIES INTO ASSETS

Believe it or not, there are some evils which threaten us that we can turn into assets. We get beyond their power when we confront them, not with resentment but with resourcefulness, and learn to use our troubles to add new dimensions to our lives. As much as we hate trouble, complain about it, and try to avoid it, what we are most thankful for as we look back over life are the things that, at the time, seemed hostile, but which, by their challenge, saved us.

Wendell Wilkie once said, 'What a man needs to get ahead is a powerful enemy." Edmund Burke said, "Our antagonist is our helper. He that wrestles with us, strengthens our muscles, and sharpens our skill."

Human nature must have something to push against and something to wrestle with. I suppose that is the hopeful thing about handicaps. We all have them in some form. Handicaps are the hard things we wrestle with and push against.

Psychiatrist Marie Ray, after making a study of the relation between handicaps and achievements, and going down the list of notable people, concluded that most of the shining lights of history were made by people who struggled against some disability or some responsibility that seemed too great for their powers.

This is strong medicine for an age trying hard to escape handicaps. Without minimizing the tragic elements of life, we have to grant that the sources of our anxieties could be allies. We get beyond the reach of their power to hurt us when we make use of them to help us. We need fear no evil in any difficulty we can turn into triumph.

This is what the apostle Paul said, looking back over the frustrations, persecutions, and tribulations he had experienced: "We are hard pressed on every side, but not crushed; perplexed, but not in despair; persecuted, but not abandoned; struck down, but not destroyed." (2 Cor. 4:8–9). Paul was saying we have learned to triumph, even in threatening circumstances.

THE EVILS THAT DESTROY

As Friedrich Nietzsche was fond to point out, "What does not destroy me, makes me stronger."[1] The problem is some evils that can destroy us.

To be sure, some evils we can kick away with our feet. Some we can wrestle with and use to sharpen our skills. But then there are those that are beyond explanation or human understanding. There seems no way around them or over them, only through the valley. For such, the only hope comes from great depths of resources from God within the believer. Only there can we find the power to get beyond the reach of their real power to destroy the spirit.

I'm thinking of sufferers who have lived a long time with pain, "The walking wounded," as someone called them. People to whom no saving miracle has come except through the bravery. The world will never know how much we owe to people who demonstrate this. There are people who have to live with the evil of this world's ill will. They are caught in the crosscurrents of human passions, racial hatred, or class wars. As they walk this bitter road they do not become bitter themselves or let the bitterness get into them.

Roland Hayes, a humble and greatly gifted African American tenor said, "My voice teacher told me that as an artist, and as a black artist, I would suffer terribly and needlessly if I allowed the barbs to penetrate my soul. But if my heart was right and my spirit divinely disciplined, then nobody in all of the world would be able to hurt me. I know now that this is true. I try every moment to live in such awareness of the presence of God that no bitterness can creep into my heart. In this way I have learned to be happy even in the discovery that nobody in the world can hurt me, except myself."

That is high ground for the human spirit. When a person reaches that point, he or she is beyond the reach of trouble.

WHAT WOULD JESUS FEAR?

This perspective is fundamentally Christian. It is Christ himself who has taught us what David, the psalmist, meant by this psalm. When he said, "I will fear no evil," he did not mean that he didn't have evil that had made its unwelcome way into his life. He did indeed experience the worst of evil.

Jesus was called a traitor, a blasphemer, an enemy of God. He was disowned, despised, rejected, a "man of sorrows and acquainted with grief." These troubles touched our Lord deeply, but they did not destroy Him. Never once was He pushed into unrighteousness. He took the evil of men and made it a lever to lift them. He took their blows and turned them into blessings until the cross on which He was crucified became the living symbol of salvation.

That is the Christian answer to the piled-up evil of the world—not a simplistic explanation, but an overcoming, a redemption.

Make this ancient word your own. It is a true word from God for all of us living in this evil world. "I will fear no evil, for You are with me."

9

CHALLENGING
ANGER

Self-driven anger is a blight; apathy is a disease.
Righteous action on justified anger demonstrates godliness.

Jesus didn't get along with everybody. That is both a comfort and a challenge. It is a comfort because we don't get along with everybody either. It is a challenge because it sets us to thinking about what the divine nature really is and what our responsibility is in relation to it.

A university president, among his many duties, was charged with the responsibility of procuring endowments for the university he served. He was eminently qualified, gifted with charm, affability, and the ability to make friends and influence people. On his faculty was a rather forthright young professor whose habit of blurting out the painful truth was often a source of embarrassment.

While the president loved the truth, of course, he was also interested in raising funds. To instruct the young professor in more democratic and diplomatic ways, he invited him to attend chapel on a particular occasion. The president spoke, in his amiable way, on the psychological methods of Jesus, emphasizing the great tact and diplomacy with which the Master always found common ground with His hearers. He showed how, through parables and with infinite, patient skill, Jesus entered the minds of listeners to persuade them to His way.

As the professor and the president left the chapel together, the young man said, "I see what you mean, sir; I shall try to profit by your address." The president smiled complacently—as it turned out, too complacently. For in the next breath the young professor said, "There is one thing, however, that bothers me. If Jesus was so beautifully tactful and diplomatic, how did He manage to get Himself crucified?"

In the story of His driving the money changers out of the temple, recorded in Matthew 21, we are given the picture of an angry Christ. Deliberately He strode into the temple to strike at the merchants there, and at the ruling classes of Jerusalem behind them—striking them where they would feel it most, in their moneybags. He knew, long ago, that this temple had ceased to serve the people it professed to serve. It was not a house of prayer, but a marketplace, a bazaar, a business.

The people knew it too. Good Jews that they were, they were heartily ashamed of it. They knew Caiaphas, the high priest, and the Sadducee clique had turned their temple into a money-making machine and that these pious leaders had little interest in the temple beyond that it offered them a lucrative source of wealth. People were being cheated and shortchanged in the house of God, and the cheaters resented Jesus' intrusion. Jesus was aware of their evil practices. It was hard to know, that morning, just who or what was being worshiped there. Was it God, or mammon, or Beelzebub?

The outer court of the Gentiles was a dirty, smelly market, noisy with the deafening clamor of sellers hawking their wares; bleating sheep; cackling, cooped-up birds; bargaining money changers; and the bellows of restless oxen. This was confusion confounded, blaspheme beyond excuse, a sacrilege to the honest seeker having come to the temple to commune with God. It wasn't a pretty picture, even when the rabbinical writers try to explain it.

Into this scene came Jesus of Nazareth, not to worship, but to destroy the false values which the noble temple now had been made to represent. He seized the whip of twisted cords, and in His eyes blazed an anger that must have struck terror in the hearts of evil people. He swept the moneybags to the floor, scattering the coins. He overturned a second table, then another and another. The wrath of God incarnate stormed through the detestable market, driving out the cattle, freeing the caged sacrificial doves, and shouting their own Scripture at the fleeing tradesmen: "'My house will be called a house of prayer,' but you are making it a 'den of robbers'" (Matt. 21:13). Then, His passion spent, He sat down amid the great pillars that led to the Holy of Holies.

What are we to make of this outburst? How do we account for this angry Christ? Did Jesus slip out of character? Did He lose His temper and become more human than divine? Does this occasion reveal an impetuosity in Him, which—had He lived longer—He would have learned to curb and control?

Or perhaps there is confusion in our minds as to the real character of His divine nature. Was Jesus less divine here, with a whip in His hands than when He stretched forth those same hands on a cross to take the nails?

In truth, the real problem with Jesus being angry is the bad theology of some Christians who refuse to accept the biblical fact that God gets angry. Perhaps their god would never get angry; their god would never inflict punishment; their god would never raise his voice. But of course, their god is not the God of the Bible—their god is an idol of their own making. Jesus was no less God when He got angry because Jesus was fully God and fully man. However He acted at any moment as a man, He was likewise acting as God. So when He was angry in that market, it was God's will, because it was Jesus' will (and vice versa).

EMOTIONS ARE NOT SIN

Hopefully, by now, most of us have outgrown the immature idea that anger is a sinful emotion. The fact is there is no sinful emotion. There are sinful uses of emotion and there are some people who misuse their God-given powers as a blundering organist might misuse a pipe organ, taking notes intended to produce fine harmony and weaving them into discord.

Anger is a powerful energy of the soul, divinely planted, closely allied to the fighting instinct, and designed, as all emotions are designed, for constructive, spiritual use. This is why God could inspire David to write a psalm affirming us "in [our] anger" and yet cautioning, "do not sin" (4:4). Paul was likewise inspired by God's Spirit to echo the same in his letter to the Ephesians (4:26). God's Word explicitly teaches it is acceptable and good on occasion to be angry, and to be in such a state without sinning.

FOOLISH AND SINFUL ANGER

Two things need to be noted about anger. The first is, anger is not, in and of itself, power. Probably the chief reason we classify anger among the vices and not the virtues is that the ordinary brands of it are expressions of human frailty and weakness.

Anger is prone to mix itself with base and unlovely elements. So frequently does it stir up the mud at the bottom of the soul that it is not easy to free our minds from the feeling that anger has something of sin in it; or if not actual sin, an unlovely flaw in conduct, a deformity in character from which we may wisely pray to be delivered.

Much of our anger is indeed weakness, not strength. It becomes uncontrolled, a response of emotional immaturity, and a sign of arrested development. So, anger in a baby is quite normal, a sign of emotional vitality. The terrible-tempered adult, however, is not a very impressive figure. He has never outgrown his childhood.

His life is a series of emotional explosions. He gets fearfully and powerfully mad. All the steam blows off in the whistle. He is not nearly so impressive as he imagines himself to be.

Proverbs pulls no punches in describing this quick-tempered person: he or she "does foolish things (14:17)" and "displays folly" (v 29). Even more to the point, "Every fool is quick to quarrel" (20:3). And Proverbs 22:24 warns, "Do not make friends with a hot-tempered [person], do not associate with one easily angered." Proverbs is offering sage and godly advice, if for no other reason than that though "a hot-tempered man must pay the penalty; if you rescue him, you will have to do it again" (19:19). The hot-tempered person not only is in a perpetual state of immaturity and self-destruction, but he or she is prone to drag down and hurt others in the vicinity as well.

BESIDE OURSELVES

During World War II, England's prime minister, Winston Churchill, once listened to a hot-tempered, raving, ranting tirade directed against him by an opponent whose might worked faster than his brain. Churchill arose and said, "Our honorable colleague should, by now, have trained himself not to generate more imagination than he has the capacity to hold." That is good advice for us all.

The fact is, much of our anger is petty, rising out of selfishness. Our feelings have been hurt, or our rights have been encroached upon, or somebody has nosed into the parking place we wanted and felt we were entitled to, and in a rage we are babies again, screaming "somebody took my rattle."

What makes you angry? That is the revealing question. As the oft-quoted proverb says, "You can tell the size of a man by the size of the thing that makes him mad."

Certainly, to boil inside; to lose control because of some trivial, personal hurt; to allow the wild forces of our being to run loose because our wills have been crossed or self-esteem has been wounded—such is not a mark of power. Rather, that is poison. And this poison destroys lives.

Beethoven is thought to have brought on his own deafness by falling into a fit of anger. Indeed, psychologists attest that the emotion of anger produces more immediate effects on the chemical balance of the body than any other emotion, including fear. While the emotion may pass swiftly, the damage does not. "It's all over in a minute," we say. Yes, but so is a cyclone. Then the wreckage has to be cleared, and that may take weeks or months; in some cases, the damage can never be undone.

SINFUL ANGER

The Bible rather consistently warns us against the sinful misuse of anger. In Christ we have the supreme example of poise and emotional control. It was said of Christ that, "When He was reviled, he reviled not again," but ruled His surging spirit after the manner of a loving God.

As a boy, Roland Hayes heard an old black minister preach a sermon on Christ before Pilate, and how they went about confronting each other. Pilate, irked by the silence of Jesus, cried, "Why don't You answer me? Don't You know I have power?"

The old preacher went on to say, "No matter how angry the crowd got, He never said a mumberlin' word—not a word."

Years later, at the peak of fame with his golden voice, Roland Hayes stood before a Nazi audience in Berlin's Beethoven Hall. The audience was hostile, ugly, scornful of a Negro daring to sing at the center of Aryan culture. He was greeted with a chorus of Nazi hisses growing louder and more ominous.

For ten minutes Hayes stood there in silence at the piano, resentment swelling up in him like an irresistible tide. Then he remembered the sermon of so long ago: "He never said a mumberlin' word. Not a word." Hayes shouted back no words born in anger. He kept his head, for he knew the ultimate power was on his side, not theirs.

He stood there and prayed silently, and the quiet dignity of his courage conquered the savage spirits in the audience. In the hushed pianissimo he began to sing a song of Schubert. He won, without saying so much as a "mumberlin' word—not a word."

Indeed, "Better a patient man than a warrior, a man who controls his temper than one who takes a city" (Prov. 16:32).

ANGER MISDIRECTED

Anger is not power when it is uncontrolled, and it is not power when it is ethically misdirected. We suffer more from misguided indignation than we do from uncontrolled passion.

Author Dr. Ralph Sockman tells of the early days of the motion picture industry when western thrillers were first shown in the ranch towns of the west. The cowboys rode in from miles around and sat down in dingy movie theaters to watch the villain as he moved across the screen shooting up the town, robbing banks, and holding the lovely heroine at his mercy.

The cowhands at times became so excited and enraged at the villain that they pulled out their guns and shot at him on the screen. They were not going to let a man get away with that. They seemed not to know that what they damaged was the movie theater furniture, not the villain. He was somewhere else. That kind of naive moral indignation is typical of much of our current social indignation.

Not too many years ago the kaiser was the villain, then it was Hitler, then Stalin, then the Vietcong, then Hussein, now the president of Iran or Syria, or the radical Muslim. Tomorrow it will be another. We manage somehow to be angry at something most of the time; and we do well to be angry because there are terrifying evils to arouse righteous resentments.

But it is easier to shoot the villains than to get at the villainy. It is easier to kill bad men than to build good democracies. If only the same emotions that we array against the villains could be directed against the causes that produce them—against the poverty, and sin, and human misery that breed the badness—what a powerful, healing, redemptive force our indignation would become.

CLEAN ANGER—CONSTRUCTIVELY, SPIRITUALLY DEDICATED

The Son of Man with the whip of cords in His hands and evil cowering before Him—that is a God-given symbol and as much a revelation of the divine nature as the cross.

Christians are not stoics who regard the human passions as forces to be held in and bottled up. Neither are we Buddhists regarding the passions as evil in us to be cast out. You should not break the spirit of a person any more than you should break the spirit of a fine-tempered horse. You must not destroy the powers that make you a person nor tame the warrior instinct in the human soul. You must not ask God to take away your temper or lessen it one whit, lest the answer to your prayers make you less a person you are and should be. You mustn't ask God to eliminate anger from your being lest you presume to condemn Him for His own righteous wrath.

All these stormy emotions of our being are divinely planted. They are nature's way of mobilizing our forces for the fight. They must not be destroyed nor suppressed, but harnessed, put to use, consecrated to the work of the kingdom of God. Clean anger gives a good boldness to the tongue. Martin Luther said, "When I am angry I preach well and pray better." Dr. Channing said, "Ordinarily I weigh one hundred twenty pounds; when I am angry, I weigh a ton."

The Congressional Medal of Honor was given to a young officer who, when the battle looked hopeless, waged what his superior officers called a one-man war. He took matters into his hands and did the fighting like a hundred men. When he was asked how he did it, he replied, "I just got angry." How many unbelievably good things have come to us because someone got angry? I have read that the dial telephone was created out of the indignation of a funeral director who was convinced operators were deliberately bungling his calls.

It would be interesting to trace back to their sources the laws protecting health and human rights and to see how many of them, from the Magna Carta down, have come because somebody got angry. English prisons were the perfect picture of a vile, filthy, disease-ridden hell on earth until John Howard and his followers got angry. Slavery was deeply entrenched in this new world until men like Garrison and early founders of The Wesleyan Church "saw in the sorrowful face of the slave the shadowed face of God." Nerved by a righteous wrath that would not be silenced, Garrison hurled his challenge in white heat: "I will not equivocate, I will not excuse, I will not retreat a single inch, and I will be heard."

A MODEL OF RIGHTEOUS ANGER

Hospitals were horrible until Florence Nightingale got angry. In a biography she is presented not as a gentle angel of mercy but as a hothouse of emotion; a stubborn, high-tempered woman with the call of God within her soul, hounding and bullying government officials into providing decent treatment for the wounded and the dying until they came to tremble at the mention of her name.

Anger is not the opposite of love. (As we saw in a previous chapter, fear is the better fit for that role—perfect love casts out fear, not anger.) Sometimes anger is the clearest expression of love. How can we love people and stand by while they are wounded and exploited by selfish and greedy men? In drug trafficking, for example, men profit by preying upon human weakness. This postmodern slave trade needs to feel the heat of our righteous indignation. One of the most lamentable weaknesses of our generation lies in its lukewarm approximation of love, and the feebleness that comes of such moderate complacency (and complicity).

Monstrous evils thrive under our noses, become entrenched in politics and custom, and grow brazenly insolent to every plea for decency and justice, because we who are Christians do not speak. We need to feel what Moses felt as he stood before Pharoah; what Jesus felt as He stood in the shameful temple court. We need to feel what Lincoln felt one day in New Orleans when he saw a slave woman sold at auction. Do not forget what he said as he stood there, tall, gaunt, and furious, his fingernails biting into his hands: "That thing called slavery is wrong, and if I ever get a chance to hit it, I'll hit it hard."

Here is the gambling octopus with a stranglehold on the nation, pushing its slimy tentacles into city, county, and state governments, and even into college athletics, and now on the Internet. Do you think that could happen except for the apathy of good people?

Robert E. Lee, about whom it has been said that "neither South nor North has produced a greater gentleman," was approached after the Civil War by the managers of the infamous Lousiana Lottery. He sat in his old rocking chair, crutches at his side, and listened to their proposition.

He could not believe his ears. In fact, he asked them to repeat their request, thinking he had not heard them right. They said they wanted no money; all they wanted was the use of his name; for that they would make him rich. Lee straightened in his chair, buttoned his gray tunic about him and thundered, "Gentlemen, I lost my home in the war. I lost my fortune on the way. I lost everything in the war except my name. My name is not for sale, and if you fellows don't get out of here, I'll break this crutch over your heads."

CLEAN PASSION UNDER CONTROL

We all could use some of that kind of anger. It is the power of a clean passion under control, directed and dedicated to the divine law in human life. The poet put it in a few powerful words:

Keep us alive, O Lord, while we live.
Arouse the sluggish forces in our being
So that we sleep not the sleep of death.
If there be a task in the church to do,
And we have the energy to do it,
Save us from the shabby excuses we make,
From spiritual laziness and listlessness.
If there be a foe to face,
May no lack of courage bow our spirit or silence or voice.
Keep ever before us the picture of an earnest Christ.[1]

10

QUELLING FATIGUE

Exhaustion dulls the senses and dims the mind;
God's prescription of Sabbath rest applies today, as much in ages past.

Everyone gets tired. One day, when the weight of the world seems terribly heavy, a mother of six slumps in her chair and says, "I'm tired; I'm tired way down into the future." And who can blame her?

We all have moments like that, perhaps more often than we want to admit. We need to be extremely watchful when such moments come, because we are not normal then, we are not ourselves. Tiredness acts like a drug. It dulls the mind, weakens the will, and makes for incoherence, loss of temper, and loss of morals.

LET MY PEOPLE REST

Sometimes tiredness affects a whole generation, spreads like an epidemic, and becomes the prevailing mood of an age. We witnessed this phenomenon in the history of the people of Israel as they journeyed from Egypt's bondage to the Promised Land. They were not themselves as they murmured against Moses. It was Moses who had led them out of bondage. He set their feet on the road to freedom. They were part of a great movement, one of the greatest in human history. Yet, from the beginning of the venture they were not behaving very well.

In incident after incident the record reveals how long years of slavery had corroded them and bleached all the fight out of them. They became tired quickly, and were easily disheartened. Every time they were confronted with a problem they panicked, grumbled, and wanted to turn back. When Pharoah's army was pursuing them, they grumbled against Moses. When the wilderness yielded grudging food, they grumbled again. When they came to Mirah and stooped to drink and found the waters brackish, they spat the water back and grumbled more.

There was an undertone of irritability; that murmuring about a lost, idealized past. They would rather be slaves in Egypt than corpses in the wilderness. Moses learned it is easier to get people out of slavery than to get slavery out of people.

In the midst of all that bickering and confusion and sweaty marching, they came to a place called Elim where there were twelve wells of water, and seventy palm trees. They encamped there by the waters. It does not take much imagination to visualize that: twelve wells of water, seventy palm trees, cool shade, green grass, rest. At Elim their faith in the goodness and mercy of God was renewed.

WE'RE TIRED

You and I have a lot in common with these ancient marchers. We too are part of a moving, marching, irritable generation. There is a kind of weariness in the atmosphere. Our daily speech is filled with words like *strain, stress,* and *tension.* The strains of life are making people sick. Dr. Paul Dudley White, President Eisenhower's personal physician, said, "Our civilization is a fatiguing one. It is too tense, too full of noise and hurry, and the most common complaint in our society is, 'I'm tired.'"

What do Christians do when we are tired. I remember the preacher who was speaking at a ministerial convention who made the comment that people are so nervous these days that it had been years since he had seen anyone fall asleep in church, and that was bad. I still see some nodding off happening in the pews these days, but the pastor's point is well (if not humorously) taken.

There are at least three types of weariness that we can trace from the ancient road of the Israelite wanderers to our modern roads.

IT'S PHYSICAL

There is the tiredness of physical exhaustion. This is probably the most familiar kind of fatigue, but really it's not that easy to explain. What is tiredness? Fatigue? Exhaustion? When you are tired, what is it that gets tired? The dictionary calls it, "depletion of energy, exhaustion of strength." We drive our muscles or our minds; we overtax our energies, and after a while a kind of uncomfortable disintegration sets in. There is a defense mechanism that nature sets up against further effort until resources of energy can be replenished. The body is an amazing piece of machinery.

Bob Hope, the late comedian, once reported his activities of the day. He said his heart beat 103,369 times, his blood traveled 168 miles, he breathed 23,040 times, he inhaled 438 cubic feet of air, he ate 3 pounds of food, and drank 2 pounds of liquid, he perspired 1 pint, he generated 450 tons of energy, he spoke 4,800 words, moved 750 major muscles, and exercised 7 million brain cells. Then he said, "Boy, am I tired."

We can all understand that kind of tiredness. It is at this point we can understand the Israelites traveling from Egypt to Canaan. The long march across the desert, day after day; the sand, the sweat, the sun. They were physically exhausted. "Then they came to Elim, where there were twelve springs and seventy palm trees, and they camped there near the water" (Ex. 15:27).

The only sure remedy for that kind of tiredness is rest, relaxation, restoration. There is an affinity between water and earth and our bodies. My physician told me on one occasion that I should have a lot of water. I agreed and replied, "Yes, I want a lot of water with a boat on it and a fishing rod in my hand." Many of our modern tensions would diminish if we could find our way to some Elim, if we could make wiser use of nature's restorative powers.

The psalmist knew there is a real connection between green pastures, still waters, and restored souls (Ps. 23).

IT'S EMOTIONAL

There is another kind of tiredness that is obvious in the traveling of the ancient Israelites to the Promised Land. There are intense emotional factors in fatigue. We all experience at times the tiredness of mental and emotional frustration and fatigue.

This is the weariness that comes from prolonged waiting, disappointment, or delayed hopes. The road to the Promised Land was longer than they thought. It was not the easy victory they had imagined. This dusty desert was not the utopia they had been expecting. They had pictured the thrill of it all, getting out of Egypt, being free, marching and singing their way to the Promised Land. They thought one good battle would do it; one leap of faith, then all their troubles would be over, in the land of promise. They had not figured on the monotony, day after dreary day, keeping at it while the sun was beating down. The desert was stretching out in front of them with no Promised Land in sight.

"The trouble with life," said Dorothy Sayers, "is that it is so everlastingly daily." Indeed, it gets in your bones after a while, this kind of tiredness, the weariness of just keeping at it, the monotony of the long road or the frustration of delayed hope. We have to face the uncomfortable truth of life that in this world there are no easy victories, no permanent victories. You win a battle today and you are in for another battle tomorrow. You must get up every day and do it again.

When I was a pastor I would rejoice over spiritual victories for the church, but they did not last. There were always new battles to fight. That is true on the world scene whether it's the race problem, cultural stresses, political issues, terrorism; we win a battle today and face one similar to it tomorrow. We are going to have to learn to live with frustration, with one crisis after another. Life consists of frayed nerves, and moral and spiritual frustration, which bring along weariness. The road to the Promised Land is much longer than many of us thought.

RENEW OUR STRENGTH

Emotional tiredness cannot be cured by rest or relaxation. This is precisely what we must not do—rest, relax, give up, quit. No. This is what our enemies are counting on. They expect to wear us down and tire us out. This kind of tiredness calls for another response, a renewal of moral courage—the courage that expects frustration, yet keeps patiently believing, that resists all temptation to feel sorry for oneself or give up the battle.

In 1891 Lord Randolph Churchill, the father of Winston, wrote a letter to his wife saying that in all probability more than two thirds of his life was over. He said he would not spend the remainder of his years beating his head against a stone wall. There had been nothing but abuse and misunderstanding, and he was tired of it all. He declared he would not continue in public life any longer. I can understand that, and I'm sure you can too. I have heard many people over the years, from ministers to mothers and fathers, say they are tired of it all.

I'm glad Moses did not talk that way in the desert. I'm glad, too, that Winston Churchill did not talk the way his father did. He must have had something his father lacked. In the dark days of

World War II when all seemed lost, the people of England were tired enough. It was at that point Winston Churchill said, "We shall fight on the beaches, we shall fight in the streets, we shall never surrender, never give up."

TENACITY

Courage—what our mothers used to call "stick-to-itiveness"—that's what God is after. So you say you're tired and going to quit. Someone said, "That's the trouble with Christians: good people get tired of being good before bad people get tired of being bad." To stay a little longer than the enemy, that's what God is after.

Pessimism is the one thing that makes no sense. It does not matter what the fight is for, whether for our health, our faith, our character, for business, or for a decent world, pessimism is the one thing that makes no sense. I remember Isaiah saying it. He was talking about that long march of the exiles. It was going to be hard, he reminded them:

> Even youths grow tired and weary,
> and young men stumble and fall;
> but those who hope in the LORD
> will renew their strength.
> They will soar on wings like eagles;
> they will run and not grow weary,
> they will walk and not be faint (40:30–31).

The apostle Paul wrote to the Galatians, "And let us not be weary in well doing: for in due season we shall reap, if we faint not" (6:9, KJV). "Faint not"—that's it; we mustn't give up.

IT'S SPIRITUAL

But do you know what makes people most tired? Do you know what takes the heart out of people? It isn't hard work, it isn't monotony, it isn't even disappointment. It's hopelessness. It's what the Bible calls unbelief, the tiredness of spiritual depression—of waning faith. People can stand almost anything as long as they believe in what they are doing. As long as the battle has meaning and we believe will eventually arrive, we can fight on. We might get tired *in* it, but we will not get tired *of* it.

Most people can bounce back and stay with it as long as they know life has purpose. But when faith in God goes, hope goes with it because life is left without the one thing out of which hope springs: the divine purposefulness of life.

You can trace it in the ancient marchers, the children of Israel on their way to the Promised Land. They murmured against Moses when they were gripped by the growing fear that they had been deceived, that this road they were on led nowhere but to a vast grave in the desert. Maybe there was no Promised Land. Perhaps there was no God to make one. Maybe God was a delusion. Maybe Moses was a fool and the adventure a mirage, a dream that had no chance of coming true. "Have you taken us away to die in the wilderness?" That's what took the heart out of them—unbelief. It depleted them. It made them weak as water. It was unbelief that kept them from entering the Promised Land.

A WEARY GENERATION

I wonder if that hasn't something to say to our tired generation. Why is so much of our literature today drenched with pessimism and dark despair about life?

In one of George Moore's novels he tells of Irish peasants during the Great Depression, who were put to work by the government of Ireland building roads. For a time the men worked well, glad to be at work. But little by little they discovered the roads they were building led nowhere. They ran out in dreary bogs and stopped. As the truth dawned on them that the roads were pointless and that they had been put to work solely to provide employment and an excuse for feeding them, the men grew listless, leaned on their shovels, and stopped singing. The point was, roads to nowhere are difficult to make. For people to work well and sing there must be a destination.

I remember an uncle who loved to chop wood. He made it a point to keep the axe sharp. "You can't enjoy chopping wood with a dull axe," he would say. "You need to see the chips fly."

PEOPLE OF DESPAIR

There is an unmistakable connection between atheism and pessimism; between this generation's secularism and its cynicism; between its loss of faith in divine purpose and its mood of despair about the future. That is why we have a tired world on our hands. We have lost our sense of mission, the sense of divine leadership. We are not sure we are going anywhere worth getting to. Even our progress has become pointless. For a person or an age to work well and to sing, there must be an end in view.

This is reason alone that one should stick with believers. They may be unsophisticated at times, they may not always be brilliant, but they believe there is a purpose to life and that they are not alone on this road.

Otherwise, what a fool Moses would have been. He thought God was in that movement and that it was going somewhere. He thought God was getting something started and that His people were not at their end but their beginning.

A few millennia have come and gone, and we have a broader perspective. There they were, murmuring marchers, part of a movement all generations since have regarded as one of the most creative of human history. It was a time when God was in their midst, performing a new work, making a new nation. It was a time when human freedom was being hammered out in the desert; yet the only contribution they had to bring was to stand around throwing dust in the air and grumbling.

GOT FAITH?

I encourage you to do what I intend to do: to remain a believer, to cling to the faith God has given me. On the one hand, it seems pessimism makes no sense at all. But on the other hand, I would be a pessimist too if it were not for Christ. (That's one reason Christ makes so much sense to me.) Christ keeps believing in people, in you, in the future, in me. Some people may be fooled because they believe too much in the finite and the limited—in themselves, or in an idol of their making that they may even call "God." Far more people get fooled because they believe too little in the one true God.

At the beginning of this chapter I referred to a mother of six who said she was tired "way down into the future." That was Julia Ward Howe, prominent American abolitionist, social activist, and poet. And that was also just plain exhaustion talking.

We all know that moment, but we must not stay in it. She didn't. Energized by faith in a divine purpose, she wrote a song that has sent people marching and their blood tingling:

Mine eyes have seen the glory of the coming of the Lord.
He is trampling out the vintage where the grapes of wrath
are stored.
He hath loosed the fateful lightning of His terrible swift
sword,
His truth is marching on.

He has sounded forth the trumpet that shall never call
    retreat.
He is sifting out the souls of men before His mercy seat.
O be swift my soul to answer Him, be jubilant my feet,
Our God is marching on.

There is no tiredness there. No fear or despair. Just the battle and the bugle and a prayer for ears to hear the sounding. The Christian life, the life of faith, has its tired times, physically, emotionally, even spiritually. In such times we must find rest for our bodies, reinforcement for our emotions, and a renewal of purpose for our souls.

11

DEBUNKING DOUBT

Doubts undermine hope and debilitate our minds;
Jesus offers evidence to one lacking in faith.

I thank God for Thomas. I have always been glad one of the first disciples was a doubter. Everyone knows his moniker, Doubting Thomas. Fair or not, the label is glued to him. Doubt was part of the makeup of this man and, if we're honest, it is ours too.

We are introduced to Thomas three times in the Bible, although we have only a glimpse each time. Each time he is speaking words of doubt. On one occasion Jesus proposed a visit to Bethany, the home of Mary, Martha, and Lazarus. The two sisters were in mourning. The disciples, knowing the dangers in the environs of Jerusalem, tried to prevent His going. Thomas was sure the end was near and rather dismal, so he said, "Let us also go, that we may die with him" (John 11:16).

Again after the Last Supper, Jesus talked about His approaching death. He told His disciples not to be troubled—since they believed in God, they therefore should believe in Him; and if they did, they would know the way to take. Thomas again was the spokesman of despondency: "How can we know the way?" he asked (John 14:5). In so many words, Jesus responded, "Hey—you know me, you know the way, in person" (v 7, paraphrased).

Predictably, three days after Jesus' death, with news spreading like wildfire that Jesus was alive, Thomas simply could not believe the rumor—this women's talk about a resurrection. Gloomily he absented himself from the others to bury his despair in brooding solitude, like a wounded dog that crawls under a house to die. Dark must have been his night as he walked outside the city. He could not see his hand in front of him. He could only see in his mind the hand with nails driven through.

Psychologists would call Thomas's experience a trauma, a sharp wound, a shock, perhaps a neurosis. Imagine what might have been in his troubled mind. It must have kept pounding around on that one thing, the print of the nails, until it was an obsession—a hand with a nail in it, that's all he could see.

THE MIND OF A DOUBTING THOMAS

One thing was sure, he would never believe again. He had seen what happens to goodness. He had feared it all along. As far as he was concerned the chapter was closed. Resurrection? Don't be silly, he could never believe that. Dead people don't rise, not when Romans kill them. And now, there he is with tears on his face, the stubborn set of the chin: "Unless I see the nail marks in his hands and put my finger where the nails were, and put my hand into his side, I will not believe it" (John 20:25).

The likes of Thomas are reading these same words on this page. More than half the world is, deep within, just like Thomas—afraid to believe. Millions of people sit in churches around the world, even on Easter Sunday, and hear the old, incredible story wishing it were so, yet fearing it is much too good to be true.

IT'S A QUESTION OF FAITH

Many people feel about faith as Alice did upon entering Wonderland. The White Queen told Alice that she was over one hundred years old. Alice said she couldn't believe that. The Queen said, "Can't you? Try again. Take a deep breath, shut your eyes. Try!" Is that what we mean by faith? Is that what preachers mean? Take a deep breath, try again? Can the mind command the mind against the facts? How can I make myself believe?

I enjoy talking to the doubter within me. Every time I do, I see something about belief I did not see when I started out in life. Belief is much less about the facts presented; it also has a lot to do with the mind's response to the facts. We all face the same facts. Some believe. Some do not. So it's not wholly in the facts. It's also something in my response. It is important for us to view both the facts in life and the variety of responses available to us.

I have learned three things relative to my responses to the facts of life that have helped me with the Thomas within. I challenge you to try them as well.

AMONG THE PEOPLE OF THE LIGHT

If you want help with your doubts, expose yourself to the light. Go back to the Thomas story. Remember that when Jesus came to His disciples that night in the upper room where they had assembled in fear, He startled them. Standing in their presence, He gladdened their hearts. "The disciples were overjoyed when they saw the Lord" (John 20:20).

When ministers want to dramatize the importance of the church, Christian fellowship, the necessity of worship, and regular habits of church attendance, they remind us that Thomas, one of the twelve disciples, was absent when Jesus came. The man who missed the moment missed the Master.

So Thomas lived for a week in dark despondency. He wasn't in the place where he most likely would meet the Lord. Thomas is the patron saint of a generation living in a moral fog because they have detached themselves from Christian fellowship, the community of believers, and what our fathers used to call "the means of grace." Some people have trouble with doubt because they do not go where the light is and so do not expose themselves to its shining.

How many people have succumbed to the lone-ranger fallacy, the popular notion that they can be good with God independent of the fellowship of believers? So superior to ordinary mortals, they need no crutch to worship God.

Some people think they can get close enough to God on golf courses or open highways, on mountains or by the lake or sea. Unfortunately, this has not produced heroic moral giants, but spiritual illiterates prone to moral slump—a generation confused, depressed, and wondering what is the matter with life.

Trying to have a relationship with God without Christ's body (the Church) is like maintaining a long-distance relationship with a spouse over the phone or by e-mail. If you're never in each other's presence, there is going to be a lack of intimacy, no matter how rich your distanced dialogue may be. When God's Word defines the church as "Christ's body," it isn't figurative speech. There is a literal sense in which Christ is uniquely manifested, personally, in the fellowship of His people. One cannot really get close to Christ and be distant from His body any more than one can get close to a spouse by getting as far away as possible from his or her body.

Husbands and wives who know the depth of true love study their spouses throughout their lifetimes. They know their respective histories, and they listen to them regularly. There is a knowledge of that loved one that takes time, effort, and presence to acquire. A love relationship with anyone is contingent upon (defined by, even) knowing about that person. It's amazing how many people imagine they can become masters in the art of faith living without knowing the real person of Christ, except what they learn by attending church twice a year, on Easter and Christmas.

If you want to cure your doubts, you have to be present. You must stand where the light is shining, in person; go where you can feed your soul on something other than your own dark thoughts. People will never get their confused thinking straightened out until they come back to where Christ's light is shining. The honest Thomas will do that. He will go where people have found the light. He will stay within the fellowship and participate with regularity in the body of faith.

Is it any wonder that the people who need the church the most are the ones who are absent from it? There are times when pastors would like to use a bit of benevolent coercion in this matter, because they know what it means to the soul.

It is doubtful if the doubter will ever become a believer when absent habitually from the fellowship.

GETTING YOUR FACTS STRAIGHT

If you want help with your doubts you must be honest with your personal issues. No matter how we try to persuade ourselves otherwise, doubt is more emotional than intellectual. It is rooted in the heart more deeply than the head. Facts are not final. Beyond the facts is interpreting facts. Facts are not the same as truth; truth is far more than mere quantifiable information. Jesus, who called himself "the Truth," cannot be reduced to cold, hard facts.

There must be a choice in the equation. Everyone must choose between interpretations of the facts.

We all face the same facts. People who believe and those who don't live in the same world, go through the same experiences, and handle the same realities. Whether we react positively in faith or negatively in doubt depends, not so much on the facts, but upon the interpretation we choose to give them. The issue of doubt then is one deep within each of us.

Why don't people respond positively in responding to reality? Often the answer relates to a moral problem. Bad living clouds the mind and blurs the facts. We live ourselves into bad thinking just as we think ourselves into bad living. Fundamentally the answer is a relationship problem. The people we associate with and to whom we give our affection influence what we believe and what we doubt. Often a low infatuation destroys a high faith.

Doubt is generally a matter of disposition. Some people naturally find it easy to believe. They are sunny and optimistic. Others are inclined to melancholy and brooding.

Two buckets went to the well one day. One said, "No matter how full I am when I leave, I always come back empty." The other said, "I'm so happy because no matter how empty I am when I come, I always go home full." Same facts—different response. Which bucket am I? Which are you?

Peter and Thomas must have gotten on each other's nerves. Peter by nature could agree quickly and believe easily. Thomas must lag behind in investigating and questioning. Peter loved the limelight; Thomas lingered in the shadows. Peter saw the doughnut; Thomas saw the hole. When Peter had dark thoughts he doubted his doubts. Thomas was suspicious even of his high hopes. There was something different in the makeup of each person.

The doubter calls unbelief realistic thinking. Critics scoff at the Christian faith for being too emotional or just wishful thinking. Christians believe because they want to believe. But that works two ways. If we are believers because we want to believe, are all unbelievers doubters because they do not want to believe? All belief is tinged with emotion. Yet, nothing in this world is as emotional as doubt. It is the bubbling to the mind's surface of all the dark thoughts and negative fears a pessimistic soul loves to feed upon.

So then, belief or doubt, it is the choice we make in response to the same facts. While we sometimes get deceived because we believe too much, more often we get cheated because we doubt too much. Why didn't Thomas believe in the resurrection of our Lord? It was not in the facts. It was something in Thomas. He consistently chose the dark side—the negative response to reality. Perhaps you do as well.

MORE THAN A FEELING

If you want help with your doubts you must believe beyond the senses. The optic nerve must not be the sole determining factor. Thomas shut his mind to all evidence of reality except what he could grasp with his senses. "Unless I put my hand into his side," is the way he put it. In reality, seeing and touching are but a small part of what we can know and with confidence believe.

Let's be fair to Thomas. Jesus, without question, loved Thomas. He called him to be a disciple knowing all about his questioning mind. I dare say Jesus loved Thomas not in spite of that doubting mind but because of it.

What's more, the rest of the disciples weren't quick to believe the eyewitness accounts of the women who saw the resurrected Jesus until they saw Him in person. And when Thomas did see Jesus in person, his response was one of true faith. "Thomas said to him, 'My Lord and my God!'" Thomas got it like few others did, or at least were willing to confess. Thomas's doubts had been wholly converted into faith.

More than any other religion, Christianity is the chief encourager of the Thomas mind. The investigative, questioning mind is accepted by the New Testament because it does not demand a blind, unreasoning (nor unreasonable) faith. Rather, it urges people to touch and prove and use every faculty of the mind to search for truth. That inquisitive spirit represents the questioning mind of science now. The Thomas mind is multiplied into chemical laboratories, agencies of research, pushing into every hidden cranny of the earth: looking, touching, testing, proving, asking. The world is indebted to Thomas people. Where would we be without that investigative mind that seeks verifiable proof?

BELIEVING ISN'T MERELY SEEING

Even so, Jesus made a fascinating response to Thomas's faithful confession—one that I think is probably just as baffling to most Christians today as it must have been to Thomas. Jesus simply said, "Because you have seen me, you have believed; blessed are those who have not seen and yet have believed" (John 20:29). Jesus seems to be indicating there is some richer blessing for those who will believe without seeing definitive, visual proof.

That blessing characterizes the church throughout the rest of history, after the disciples' generation. All subsequent generations of Christians (including you and me) have believed in Him without ever seeing Him. Since we know no other scenario, we can't fully appreciate the blessing of believing without seeing, but Jesus says there is one.

Even so, we have a hard time believing in any advantage to belief without seeing. We still tend to be like Thomas. We want proof of God's work, and we put conditions upon God's love and sovereignty—in so many words still declaring we want to put our fingers in Jesus' wounds, and then we'll believe. God does provide signs; He answers prayers; and He performs miracles. But how often are we getting lesser blessings in the process?

Likewise, how far can science really take us into the higher nature of reality? How far can the eye see? How much do the senses tell us about God, life, and death? We cannot see air, yet we know it exists. We cannot actually look at an atom, yet we can show evidence of it.

We are grateful for the senses, those wonderful gateways through which the physical world invades our consciousness. But frankly, they're overrated. In this age of conspiracy theories and digital special effects, intelligent people know that seeing should not be a condition for believing. Those who want to insist that seeing is believing are perhaps the best marks for a con—because magicians and con men (and women) are masters at manipulating us through our senses.

Furthermore, in our digital world there are myriads of convincing visual effects that have no more reality than strings of zeros and ones inside a computer's memory. We call them "virtual realities." And they give us all the more cause for doubting our senses.

Most of the reality we know, as scientists are now demonstrating, is in a higher, invisible realm, beyond sense perception. Paul affirmed this 2,000 years ago. "So we fix our eyes not on what is seen, but on what is unseen. For what is seen is temporary, but what is unseen is eternal" (2 Cor. 4:18).

People who don't believe until they can touch and see live in a small, deceptive world. Thomas thought that, at least, he could trust his senses—that what he could see and touch he could believe. But we have learned how deceptive the senses are and how little they can grasp. Our senses cannot grasp enough of anything to give us the whole truth about anything.

THE HOPE OF HALLELUJAH

London never witnessed a funeral service quite like that of the famous preacher F. B. Meyer. Christ's Cathedral was packed with thousands of saddened people there to mourn his death. It didn't happen. There was no mourning, not a word of sorrow.

The Scriptures read were the great words of eternal life and, as the organ began to play at the conclusion of the service, the vast audience stood with bowed heads waiting for the customary funeral march. It didn't come. Instead the organ pealed out the majestic strains of the "Hallelujah Chorus." The words rang clear: "And He shall reign forever and ever."

That is our faith. We believe what we cannot see. We trust in Christ beyond the horizon. We believe His goodness beyond our sight. We trust His Word against the optic nerve. Our evidence is not in what we see or hear, nor what we could put our finger on (or in). It consists of something in another dimension of the spirit, where faith transcends reason—not contrary to it, but beyond it. That's faith: to believe in the personal God-man, Jesus, whom we cannot see.

Is your name Thomas? Are you having difficulty with your doubts. Go where the light is shining—be present. Choose carefully how you respond to facts. And believe beyond your finite senses.

12

CONQUERING
DEPRESSION

Occasional dark valleys are common to all mortals.
In moments of darkness, God enters our misery to bring hope.

hat constitutes *normality*? The word has a great deal of elasticity in it. Normal does not mean perfection. If it did, no one would be normal. It does not mean average. I am six feet two inches tall, and I have a friend who is five feet five inches tall—we both think we are normal, and most of our friends agree. There are reasonable variations between normal people in weight, height, and mental capacity. That's normal.

In the delicate area of temperament and emotional behavior, this is also true. There is no sharp, clear-cut distinction between normal and abnormal. We are all neurotic, at least in the sense that we all have nerves. We all have normal emotions, and yet sometimes those emotions behave abnormally. We all have ups and downs; good days and bad days. Everyone feels depressed sometimes.

Even so, there is that shadowy borderland between normal and abnormal, that fuzzy, halfway place where normal people have trouble with rather extraordinary emotions, and occasionally they find themselves going down into the depths and slipping into the cold, dark pool of what emotionally ill people must experience continually. Perhaps you are there now, or have been recently.

As with any chronically ill person, deeply persistent depression should be dealt with by a professional healer. But we want to address those who occasionally slip into dark valleys of irrational and unexplainable depression. Many can resonate with poet Alfred Lord Tennyson's lament, "Tears, idle tears, I know not what they mean, / Tears from the depth of some divine despair / Rise in the heart, and gather in the eyes." This seemingly meaningless depression elicits reactions and responses that, as far as we can tell, have no discernable cause. We don't know what the tears mean. But there they are.

ENTERING INTO MISERY

Picture an imaginary line running horizontally through life. Below the line is darkness, above the line, light. William James, the famous psychologist, defined this threshold as "a symbolic designation from the point at which one state of mind passes into another." Above that line we control our emotions. We have ups and downs within that realm, but we know and can handle our moods. When we dip below that line, we are in trouble. We do not now control our emotions; they control us. We are at the mercy of our moods.

That misery line varies in different people just as the pain line varies. Some can endure enormous amounts of pain, while others' pain threshold is low. But in all of us there is a line below which we are at the mercy of our moods. The more sensitive we are, the more susceptible we are. Beethoven, Tolstoy, Samuel Johnson, Abraham Lincoln, even the psalmist David—gifted, conscientious people have crossed that line.

It's interesting to discover the names given to this experience. Bunyan called it "the slough of despond." To Saint John of the Cross is was "the dark night of the soul." The military version is "battle fatigue." To the psychiatrist it might be "anxiety neurosis." The minister sums it up as "ministerial burnout," while the layman refers to it as "nervous exhaustion." The psalmist most poignantly described his state with the words, "Out of the depths I cry to you, O LORD" (Ps. 130:1).

PHYSICAL AFFLICTIONS

How does this happen to us? There is not a single or simple answer. Bodily illness can produce that run-down feeling. We are both body and mind beings, both chemically-driven animal and image-of-God spiritual. What affects the one influences the other.

Physical vitality, when depleted, can cause emotional and spiritual disorders. Chemical deficiencies through malnutrition, anemia, or glandular imbalance (to specify just a few) may be the beginning of an emotional tailspin. Low spirits are often the result of low physical vitality.

Tensions also may produce depression. Civilization's three major killers are not heart disease, cancer, and accidents, but calendars, telephones, and clocks. It's the tyranny of the accelerated life.

There is an office building, or at least there used to be, in Detroit called "ulcer alley." People there drove themselves beyond their power to endure.

Millions are living in subconscious fear, worry about jobs, health, getting old, and failing in life. The more they worry, the more they undo their capacity to cope.

MORAL FAILURES

Many people have dipped below the misery line and wonder why they feel they have lost their grip. There is a vague uneasiness about them. They feel physically weak. They simply have dipped into the realm where emotions, meant to be the driving force of life, have become the destroying force.

Ethical conflict, too, can produce depression—the indecision between what we want to do and what we ought to do. Every human soul has written deep into it God's moral standard about sex, adultery, betrayal, lies, and cruelty. We all know when we fall short.

We have swung away from these standards—but we cannot avoid them. We call them relative or irrelevant. We boast about our new freedom only to find that our consciences won't be easily dismissed; that right and wrong are not old ideas in a musty book. They are written in us, in our natures, in our subconscious minds. The sense of guilt is drawing us into a sick despondency.

A young woman came into my office one day when I was president of the college she was attending. I learned from the dean of students that she had been complaining of being ill for some time and that she had been sent to the hospital for a thorough exam. The doctors could not find what was wrong and sent her back to her college dorm.

She slumped in the chair across from my desk and said, "President Wilson, I know what's wrong with me." I was interested to hear what she had to say because it appeared we would have to send her home in the hopes her parents could discover her problem and treat her accordingly.

You can imagine how shocked I was when she said, "I am living a double life. Everyone at this Christian college thinks I am one thing, but I know I am another. I have been walking down both sides of the moral and ethical street, and it is pulling me apart. I am both physically sick and emotionally depressed because of my double life." The ethical and moral conflicts to which she subjected her mind, soul, and body were making her physically ill. In how many people is this story repeated?

ENDURING DESPONDENCY

There are other causes of emotional depression—heredity, shock, prolonged illness, bereavement, even a change of life. The question is, how do we get up? How do we Christians deal with ourselves until we are emotionally healthy? Here are some things you should do, if you find yourself in the depths of despair.

THIS SHALL PASS

Never accept any present mood as permanent. What you have, if you are down, is not unusual, it is not fatal, and it is not permanent. You are not losing your religion, your soul, or your mind. By the way, if you are attempting to help a person who is down, don't tell that person to snap out of it. That's the one thing he or she cannot do. Likewise don't declare there is nothing wrong, that it's all in the mind. It is in the feelings, and emotion is often more powerful than thought.

Fortunately in some respects our moods are fickle. Where I live, they have a saying: "If you don't like the weather, wait a minute." That is the first thing you must do: wait; realize that while right now you are under a cloud, behind the cloud the sun still shines, and one day you will be out in the clear again.

SHARE YOUR HEART

The next thing you must do is talk it out with someone. We all need an audience at times. So, talk it out to somebody you can trust. Not to everybody or just anybody, lest you make yourself vulnerable to the careless. Find someone wholesome and skilled who will provide a listening and understanding ear, and get your troubles up and out before him or her.

There was a popular song that said, "Pack up your troubles in an old kit bag and smile, smile, smile." This kind of denial is the worst thing you can do—it's certainly not biblical advice. It is not helpful to pack up your troubles in the kit bag of your unconscious self. Hold them up to the light. Vent them in the presence of some person you can trust. Not to a negative person lest they make you feel worse, but to a wholesome, positive, mentally healthy person who is a believer (of course, not all believers possess these attributes, so choose carefully). Scriptures teach us that this emotional sharing is what the body of Christ should be all about: "Carry each other's burdens, and in this way you will fulfill the law of Christ" (Gal. 6:2).

USE TOOLS

Next, work out some tension-reducing device. If your descent into the depths has been caused by tensions or faulty thinking about yourself, the way out is through straight thinking, a release from tensions and anxiety. If the problem has come about because of wrong habits, the cure lies in developing right habits. And this does not happen in a moment.

If you have been a worrier, tying yourself in a nervous knot for thirty years, don't expect to untie the knot in thirty minutes. No ecclesiastical pliers can reach in and untangle the crossed wires.

I suggest you analyze each problem causing you anxiety, one by one. Having done that, close the gate to it as deliberately as you would close the gate to the backyard.

EYES ON THE LORD

Link your emotions with positive thoughts about the power and goodness of God. There is nothing quite as important as this. Some practicing psychologists have seen this happen in their patients. One noted physician remarked, "I am convinced that the Christian religion is one of the most valuable and potent influences that we possess for producing that harmony and peace of mind and that confidence of soul which is needed to bring health and power to a large portion of nervous patients." Indeed, if you are going to rest, you need something to rest back upon.

William James was perhaps the most famous pioneer of American psychology. What is not so well known is that at age twenty-eight he suffered an almost complete breakdown of health. He was torn with doubts and afraid of life, obsessed with the horror of ending up in an asylum. He dreaded being left alone. Because of that experience he had every reason to understand emotional depression.

Later he quoted an evangelist friend, Henry Aline, who had been through a similar experience. "The fear was so invasive and powerful that if I had not clung to Scripture texts like, 'The eternal God is my refuge' or 'I am the resurrection and the life,' I think I would have gone really insane."

It is not enough for you to relax; you must relax your soul in God. Rest back on the everlasting arms and a ton of care will drop from your shoulders when you let yourself go in God.

EYES AWAY FROM YOU

Set for yourself some reasonable program of action. There is a connection between the head, the heart, and the hand. The hand is the best invention ever devised to get your attention off yourself. Some of us never manage to do that. Many turn their thoughts inward forever, feeling their pulse, analyzing every muscle twitch.

Consider how absurd the following experiment would be: The next time you drive a car, pay no attention to what is going on outside the car bur rather keep your eye on the instrument panel or dashboard. After all, the dashboard will tell you a number of things going on inside your car, important things. You can discover how your oil pressure is and whether the motor is running hot or cold or just right. Some cars have gauges that record the amount of air in each tire, or whether the windshield cleaning fluid is low or not. Just give your full attention to the dashboard and not the windshield, and see how you get along. (I predict you will end up in a ditch or in the trunk of someone else's car.)

Likewise, giving almost total attention to yourself and looking inwardly most of the time will land you in some emotional ditch (or trunk). Develop some occupational interest to get yourself off your mind and your mind off yourself. A person never does so poorly for himself when he is thinking too much about himself.

HELP SOMEBODY ELSE

There is no better medicine in the world than the stimulating tonic of love. I'm not thinking so much of what it means to those on whom it is bestowed but to the person who bestows it.

Love is the great healing emotion. It casts out fear. It cures and conquers evil. It opens channels through which God's healing Spirit flows. As a poet penned, "Seldom can the heart be lonely, if it seeks a lonelier still. / Self-forgetting, seeking only, emptier cups of love to fill."[1]

The best way to get yourself up is to help somebody else up.

While the steps I have outlined can be accomplished with some discipline and effort, much of what I have suggested is not possible without the healing power of Christ is one's life. He is the Great Physician. I have only stated in other words the great spiritual rules of wholeness which Christ taught.

Dr. James Tucker Fisher was a well-known psychiatrist. He studied under Freud, and for half a century pioneered in the field of psychiatric medicine. Near the close of his book, *A Few Buttons Missing,* he makes this summary:

> What was needed, I felt sure, was some new and enlightened recipe for living a sane and satisfying life . . . a recipe compounded from all the accumulated scientific knowledge acquired through study and research. I dreamed of writing a handbook that would be simple, practical, easy to understand, easy to follow. It would tell people how to live, what thoughts and attitudes and philosophies to cultivate, and what pitfalls to avoid in seeking mental health. I attended

every symposium it was possible for me to attend. I noted, too, the wise words of my teachers and colleagues who were leaders in their field. Then, quite by accident, I discovered that such a work had already been completed. For example, I believe the following to be true. If you were to take the sum total of all the authoritative articles ever written by the most qualified psychologists and psychiatrists on the subject of mental hygiene. If you were to combine them and refine them and cleave out the excess verbiage. If you were to take the whole of the meat and none of the parsley. And if you were to have these unadulterated bits of pre-scientific knowledge concisely expressed by the most capable of living poets, you would have an awkward and incomplete summation of the Sermon on the Mount. And it would suffer immeasurably through comparison.[2]

For nearly two thousand years the Christian world has been holding in its hands the complete answer to its restless and fruitless yearnings.

> Down in the human heart crushed by the tempter,
> Feelings lie buried that grace can restore.
> Touched by a loving heart, wakened by kindness,
> Chords that were broken can vibrate once more.

NOTES

CHAPTER 6
1. I am indebted to the thoughts of Craig Bubeck in composing this section.

CHAPTER 7
1. "From Noon of Joy to Night of Doubt," (1871), by John Campbell Shairp.
2. Quoted from "A Worker's Prayer," *Text of Poetical Works*, 2 vols., ed. Maria V. G. Havergal, (James Nisbet & Co., 1884) Il.

CHAPTER 8
1. Friedrich Nietzsche, *Twilight of the Idols,* 1888.

CHAPTER 9
1. J. Wallace Hamilton, *The Power of Anger* (Westwood, N.J.: Fleming H. Revell Co.), 123.

CHAPTER 12
1. Frances Ridley Havergal: English poet and hymn writer.
2. James Tucker Fisher, *A Few Buttons Missing* (Philidelphia, Pa.: J. B. Lippincott Co., 1951).

SMALL GROUP STUDY GUIDE

1

BEATING FRUSTRATION

WHAT DO YOU THINK?

What is your biggest pet peeve?

a. Traffic

b. In-laws

c. Coworkers

d. E-mail spam

e. Stupid bumper stickers

OUR SPIRITUAL STRUGGLE

1. What is the greatest frustration you are facing?

2. Describe how it feels when someone lets you down.

3. How do you tend to behave when you are feeling frustrated?

4. In what ways has frustration been a barrier to intimacy with God in your life?

WHAT THE BIBLE SAYS

1. Read Matthew 5:1–11. What are the typical attributes Jesus describes for His followers?

2. Dr. Wilson writes, "You can experience a new life." Do you think that's true? Why or why not?

3. Do you agree that our greatest aspirations define our character? Why or why not?

4. The author used the example of David not having the opportunity to build God's temple to demonstrate a godly pattern of responding to frustration. How does David's example apply to you? With which of his responses do you most resonate?

LIVING A HOLY LIFE

1. What attempts have you made at coping with the spiritual effects of frustration? What have been the results?

2. Which of the classic spiritual disciplines—things like prayer, Scripture study, contemplation, fasting, and silence—do you think would be most helpful in coping with frustration?

3. List some positive statements or affirmations someone who is dealing with frustration might call to mind. (For example, "I can do all things through Christ who gives me strength.")

4. What advice would you give a friend who is facing a frustrating situation?

TRY THIS!

Assess your greatest frustrated hope, vision, or plan. Assuming God's hand is at work even in a blocked heart's desire, write a letter to God describing what you intend to do to lay a foundation for someone else to accomplish your goal.

2

FINDING GOOD
IN DISAPPOINTMENTS

WHAT DO YOU THINK?

a. How do you condition your body and mind for a new day?

b. An aerobic workout

c. A good hot shower

d. A stiff cup of java

e. A favorite song on the iPod

f. A moment of prayer

OUR SPIRITUAL STRUGGLE

1. How does Christ's promise of "abundant life" jibe with your experience?

2. Have you considered the idea of preparing for failure? How does your mind resonate with that?

3. How do popular media portray the message that we are the masters of our own destiny? When have you believed that lie and been disappointed?

4. When have you settled for something less, only to find out later that what you "settled for" was better?

WHAT THE BIBLE SAYS

1. Dr. Wilson asks, "What is God's answer to life's severe disappointments?" How would you have answered before reading the chapter? How has reading about the apostle Paul adjusted your answer?

2. Read Romans 8:28. How does a right understanding of "in all things God works for the good" resonate with your experience?

3. Read Hosea 2:15, and comment on how a valley of defeat can become a door of hope.

4. How could Paul, writing from a prison cell, encourage Philippian believers (and himself) to "rejoice in the Lord, always" (Phil. 4:4)?

LIVING A HOLY LIFE

1. Consider the statement that our purpose is to "glorify God and enjoy Him forever." How can you enjoy God through pain and failure?

2. How do you respond to the idea that the weights of life bring about great triumphs? When has this been true in your life?

3. How would you respond to those who contend that God has only comfort and prosperity for true believers?

4. What may God be allowing in your life today that, while disappointing, is conditioning you for something He has for your good future?

TRY THIS!

When you are tempted to complain about a disappointing turn of events, think of Buddy in his wheelchair. Prayerfully determine you'll have an attitude like his—then put it into practice.

3

OVERWHELMED
BUT HOPEFUL

WHAT DO YOU THINK?

When you have problems, where do you go first to solve it?

a. A self-help book or guru

b. A website on the subject

c. A coworker or friend

d. A Bible teacher

e. God's Word

OUR SPIRITUAL STRUGGLE

1. Paint a word picture that takes the concept of being *overwhelmed* and makes it tangible.

2. When have you tried to solve your own problems? What has been the result? Why do humans inevitably fail at trying to take charge of our world?

3. What changes in the past year threaten to overwhelm you?

4. How do you respond to the information glut that invades life daily?

WHAT THE BIBLE SAYS

1. Read Isaiah 45:11–12. What challenge do you find in the fact that the Creator alone has the answer to life's questions?

2. Dr. Wilson says, "Nothing takes the anxiety out of life quite so much as a consciousness of God's nearness." How does this resonate with your experience?

3. Revisit Psalms 31:24; 33:20; 33:22; 71:5; 130:5. How do these statements of faith affect your feelings about your circumstances?

4. How does a mind guarded by God's peace (Phil. 4:6–7) look different from a mind fixed on earthly things? Which would you rather have?

LIVING A HOLY LIFE

1. How are you challenged by the models of godly believers who have responded well to adversity, setbacks, and overwhelming situations?

2. Why is it ultimately damaging to cut back on time with fellow believers when life is most overwhelming?

3. When you think about a future in heaven with Christ, how does this affect your mood? Why?

4. Consider the list in Philippians 4:8 of the things Paul encourages the believer to think about. List three things that fall into each category—and decide to think about those things the next time you feel overwhelmed.

TRY THIS!

This week, apply the counsel to find a small, manageable project and complete it. Then celebrate the feeling of accomplishment that comes with its completion.

4

OVERCOMING WORRY

WHAT DO YOU THINK?

John Haggai said, "You could write on countless American gravestones the epitaph: 'Hurried, Worried, Buried.'" Whom do you know whose demise may have been advanced by a lifetime of worry?

OUR SPIRITUAL STRUGGLE

1. The Greek word we translate as *worry* means "to divide the mind." How can a pattern of worry divide a mind?
2. How would you define relaxation? When was the last time you relaxed?
3. When has your "short fuse of temper" been lit by the "smoldering coals of worry"? How do you wish you would have responded instead?
4. How can a feeling of aloneness multiply your sense of worry? Why?

WHAT THE BIBLE SAYS

1. How is the ultimate cause of worry related to a lack of faith (Matt. 6:30)?
2. What does it mean to you for Jesus to invite you to trade your troubled heart for trust in Him (John 14:1)?

3. Consider and discuss why the wise writer of Proverbs would equate venting anger indiscriminately with the behavior of a fool.

4. How would a mind transformed by God (Rom. 12:2) respond to the worry-inducing situations of contemporary life?

LIVING A HOLY LIFE

1. Dr. Wilson suggests we streamline our activities and weed out those things that just don't matter. Realistically, what could (or should) you weed out?

2. In what instances in the past month might Jesus have reminded you, as He did the disciples, not to worry (Matt. 6:34)?

3. When have you found freedom from worry by focusing on something or someone outside yourself—or by focusing on God?

4. Who are two trustworthy friends or family members who can support you (and whom you can support) through trouble?

TRY THIS!

Every morning this week, read a portion of Jesus' Sermon on the Mount (Matt. 5–7). Before the end of each day put into practice at least one lesson you gleaned from your reading.

5

STILLING RESTLESSNESS

WHAT DO YOU THINK?

Sit for thirty seconds without speaking or moving. Then discuss how hard it was (or how alien it felt) to do nothing and say nothing during those moments.

OUR SPIRITUAL STRUGGLE

1. Is restlessness an external or internal problem? Give an example to support your answer.
2. Dr. Wilson says, "It is not our changing circumstances but our unregulated desires that rob us of peace." Do you agree or disagree? Why?
3. What desires of your heart remain unfulfilled? What choices are you making daily in your responses to them?
4. What would it take to bring peace and calmness to your mind? How often do you experience these treasured emotions?

WHAT THE BIBLE SAYS

1. Give examples of what it means in daily life to "delight yourself in the Lord" (Ps. 37:25). How is this contrary to the world's way?

2. Why do you suppose David and his son Solomon came to such different conclusions about life? What made the difference in David's perspective? Where did Solomon go wrong?

3. How does seeking God with a whole heart change a person's perspective and purpose?

4. What does it mean to you personally to "commit your way to the Lord" (Ps. 37:5)?

LIVING A HOLY LIFE

1. How would life change if you daily made a conscious decision to "commit your way to the Lord"?

2. How can you make delighting in the Lord a practiced habit in your life?

3. If tranquility is your desire, where does seeking God's will for your life come into play? How are the two intertwined?

4. What is the difference between lazy inaction and the decision not to move until God directs? How can we discern God's direction?

TRY THIS!

In your moments with God this week, determine to spend at least as much time silently listening for His direction as you do in speaking your desires and requests to Him.

6

CONQUERING
FEAR

WHAT DO YOU THINK?

What was your greatest fear in childhood? How did you learn to face that fear? Was it grounded in fact or fiction?

OUR SPIRITUAL STRUGGLE

1. What's the difference between a healthy fear and a phobia? Give an example of a fear turned to phobia.

2. When has your body's built-in "fight or flight" mechanism been useful in your self-preservation?

3. Can you name a fear (other than those the author names) that has driven us to explore or research?

4. Consider the phrase, "light makes the difference." When has the light of knowledge allayed your fear?

WHAT THE BIBLE SAYS

1. Why can John say unequivocally, "There is no fear in love" (1 John 4:18)? How can this be possible?

2. What is the difference between that phrase and the psalmist's contention, "The fear of the Lord is the beginning of wisdom" (Ps. 111:10)? How can they both be true?

3. How would you define "perfect love"? How does God model this for us? How can we exhibit it back to Him?

4. How can knowing the truth (and the Truth—as in John 14:6) beat back unhealthy fear?

LIVING A HOLY LIFE

1. Of what are you most afraid today? What does God's Word have to say about that fear? How does remembering that truth make you feel?

2. When you read about Jesus' frequent instructions to His followers to "fear not," what do you hear Him saying to you about the things you most fear?

3. The next time an unwelcome diagnosis or a frightful event enters your life, how will you respond? How is this different from your usual response?

4. How can you help those around you come to know the perfect love that casts out fear?

TRY THIS!

Make a list for the children in your life of things that are good to fear and things they need not fear. In age-appropriate ways, explain these to the children using a loving tone and soothing words.

7

COMFORTING TROUBLE

WHAT DO YOU THINK?

Describe the most comfortable chair you own. What gives it that distinction?

a. Its softness
b. Its shape
c. Its style
d. Its location

OUR SPIRITUAL STRUGGLE

1. When has *comfort* seemed more like a spiritual anesthetic than a gift from God? Has that brand of comfort helped or hindered your spiritual growth?

2. Where do you go for comfort? Give examples of how that has worked for you.

3. What caution could you offer to the hedonist, the stoic, or the utopian optimist?

4. Within your family and friends, name one person who (like Paul) has earned the right to be an example of God-given comfort.

WHAT THE BIBLE SAYS

1. Comment on the kind of comfort that calls us to be equipped for spiritual battle, not made at ease in a shallow existence.

2. Consider the synonyms of *Paraclete* listed in the chapter. What do they add to your understanding of the Holy Spirit's role?

3. Read Jesus' promise of the Holy Spirit (John 14:15–18). How can this Counselor (also called the Comforter) transform a believer's life?

4. In 2 Corinthians 12:9 Paul writes, "[Christ's] grace is sufficient." How can His grace be sufficient for a believer who had experienced the trials Paul had?

LIVING A HOLY LIFE

1. In what areas of life do you feel the need for your spent resources to be replenished by the God of all comfort?

2. How would you characterize your life before Christ? What comfort do you find in the reminder of God's grace in saving you from a life of sin and regret?

3. Read Hebrews 12:1–4. What comfort can you find in the sufferings Christ endured? How does considering what He endured challenge and uplift you?

4. What comfort can you draw from Christ's victory over sin, death, and the grave? How can His resurrection be a source of your consolation?

TRY THIS!

Find a friend, coworker, or family member who needs comfort. This week, find at least two practical ways to reflect God's comfort to that person.

8

PERSEVERING THROUGH AFFLICTION

WHAT DO YOU THINK?

What kinds of insurance do you carry? Why do, in essence, place a bet that bad things will happen to you?

OUR SPIRITUAL STRUGGLE

1. Describe a time when you felt God's nearness most palpably. Was it in a time of ease or a time of trouble? Why?
2. When have you been able to turn a trouble into an asset? How was this possible?
3. Dr. Wilson cites Nietzches's famous phrase, "What does not destroy me, makes me stronger." What are some of the evils that have the potential to destroy a person?
4. List some of the many dangers we might be tempted to underestimate—and thus fall prey to.

WHAT THE BIBLE SAYS

1. When do you typically hear Psalm 23 read aloud? When you read v 4 in light of the evils we might reasonably fear in modern life, how does it comfort you?
2. Of what practical help to you is God's promised nearness?

3. Read 2 Corinthians 4:8–9, replacing your own struggles with those the apostle faced. Point to a trouble you've experienced that pressed, but did not destroy you.

4. How did Satan's attacks on Jesus on earth work for our ultimate good and God's eternal glory? Why is this the ultimate example of turning troubles into assets?

LIVING A HOLY LIFE

1. What troubles do you believe have handicapped you? What will you do now, rather than considering them handicaps?

2. How would you define bravery in light of this chapter's observations?

3. Who are the people who would try to trip you up and steal God's joy from you? How will you respond the next time you encounter them?

4. What are some suggestions on ways to keep a bitter road from turning your spirit to bitterness?

TRY THIS!

On a card or sheet of parchment paper, handwrite the words of Psalm 23:4. Then place it somewhere you pass every day—and read it to remind yourself of God's nearness.

9

CHALLENGING ANGER

WHAT DO YOU THINK?

Psychologist Jan Silvious likens anger to "Mt. Vesuvius erupting." When has someone else's Vesuvius lava erupted all over you?

OUR SPIRITUAL STRUGGLE

1. With whom did Jesus get along? With whom did He not get along?
2. Dr. Wilson says, "Anger is prone to mix itself with base and unlovely elements." Explain how this happens.
3. Give an example of each: anger expressing a human weakness; anger expressing a human strength.
4. What is the connection between a person who indiscriminately spews anger and one the writer of Proverbs would classify as a "fool"?

WHAT THE BIBLE SAYS

1. How do you respond to the picture of an angry God incarnate in the scene where Jesus overturned the tables in the temple?
2. Was Jesus less divine when He was expressing anger than when He was meekly allowing the Roman soldiers to crucify Him? Why or why not?

3. Read Ephesians 4:26 and discuss Paul's admonition of not letting the sun go down on our anger.

4. What is the difference between directing our anger at a villain and directing our anger against the causes that produce villains? Which is more constructive? Why?

LIVING A HOLY LIFE

1. In the past month, what are the things that have made you angry? Which were righteous causes? Which were selfish?

2. What is it about anger that can cause us to sin? What is it about anger that can actually lead us to righteous action?

3. What are some of the constructive, spiritual uses we might find for anger in daily life? How can we recognize them?

4. What are some biblically sound ways of controlling our tempers?

TRY THIS!

This week, when you encounter injustice in your circle of influence or the world at large, allow yourself to become righteously angry to the point of worthwhile action.

10

QUELLING FATIGUE

WHAT DO YOU THINK?

What is your favorite thing to do when you're exhausted?

a. Soak in a Jacuzzi tub

b. Escape in a good novel

c. Curl up on a cushy couch

d. Hit the gym for a workout

e. Grab the TV remote and zone out

OUR SPIRITUAL STRUGGLE

1. How often have you characterized yourself as stressed, strained, or exhausted in the last week? How often have you heard others do the same?

2. In what ways does exhaustion affect your mood? What impact does it have on your faith in God?

3. Dr. Wilson asks, "What do Christians do when we're tired?" How would you answer that? What *should* we do?

4. Explain the differences between physical, emotional, and spiritual fatigue? Why is it necessary for us to recognize the cause before trying to find a solution?

WHAT THE BIBLE SAYS

1. Why do you suppose the psalmist pointed out that God's path offers "green pastures, still waters and restored souls"?

2. Read Isaiah 40:31. What does the prophet mean by "hope in the Lord"? How can this refresh a tired heart?

3. Explain what spiritual depression or exhaustion looks like. What are its causes?

4. Read Proverbs 29:18. How does having God's vision energize and excite you?

LIVING A HOLY LIFE

1. When have you awakened from a good night's sleep but still felt exhausted? Was your remaining fatigue physical, or more likely emotional or spiritual?

2. How does the monotony of daily life drain you emotionally? What do you think God's Word would prescribe as an antidote?

3. In what exhausting areas of life do you need Winston Churchill's resolve to "never give up"? Where will you find that tenacity to press on?

4. What is the destination of your life? Why is it crucial for you to have a goal to work toward?

TRY THIS!

Even if you've never done it before, go to prayer this week and ask God for His vision, His purpose for your life. Listen for His answer—and act on that purpose every day.

11

DEBUNKING DOUBT

WHAT DO YOU THINK?

Discuss your response to the following quote from V. Raymond Edman: "Don't doubt in the dark what God has revealed in the light."

OUR SPIRITUAL STRUGGLE

1. How would you define faith? Why does it matter where you place your faith?
2. Is doubt the opposite of faith? Or is it something else?
3. What are some facts that have led you to believe? Why do you suppose others, when faced with the same facts, make a different choice?
4. How can being in the presence of believers impact a doubter's mood and thoughts?

WHAT THE BIBLE SAYS

1. What difference does the presence of Christ make to a doubting heart? Even though we cannot see Him physically, how can we be sure He is near? (For clues read John 20:20.)
2. Read Hebrews 10:25 to hear an admonition to cluster together with other believers. Why is the writer so insistent on this point?

3. Dr. Wilson insists we must "go where you can feed your soul on something other than your own dark thoughts." How do you respond to that statement? Why?

4. What do you suppose Jesus means when He tells Thomas, "Blessed are those who have not seen, and yet have believed" (John 20:29)

LIVING A HOLY LIFE

1. How do you interpret the facts of Christ's death and resurrection—personally?

2. What relationships do you need to get right in order to be a stronger believer (and less of a Thomas)?

3. What does it mean for a believer to "fix our eyes not on what is seen, but on what is unseen" (2 Cor. 4:18)?

4. What would you say to a doubter who says your faith is emotion-based wishful thinking?

TRY THIS!

Make a list of the questions that dog your faith. Discuss them with your pastor or mature fellow believers, and search the Scriptures for God's perspective on them.

12

CONQUERING
DEPRESSION

WHAT DO YOU THINK?

According to the Mayo Clinic: "Mild depression often can be improved with self-care that enhances physical and mental well-being." What has helped lift you out of "down days" of mild depression?

OUR SPIRITUAL STRUGGLE

1. How do your experiences jibe with the author's observation that the most sensitive and creative among us are more susceptible to depression?
2. When have your emotions dipped "below the line" to become a destroying force in your life? Why?
3. Why would guilt contribute to someone's depression? How are these emotions interrelated?
4. Why is it helpful for us to remind ourselves that moods aren't permanent? How can this raise us out of mild depression?

WHAT THE BIBLE SAYS

1. When have you cried to the Lord out of the depths (Ps. 130:1)? How do you know He heard you?

2. Review Galatians 6:2 and discuss how you've been helped by someone shouldering your burden. How can you do the same for someone else?

3. List all the Scriptures you can think of that describe the power of God. Do the same for those about His goodness.

4. How do Jesus' "blessed are . . ." statements in the Beatitudes (Matt. 5:3–12) turn human wisdom upside down?

LIVING A HOLY LIVING

1. Return to your list of Scriptures on the power and goodness of God. How do these aspects of His character encourage you?

2. When has God's Spirit been to you the Great Physician of body, heart, and soul?

3. Dr. Wilson says love "opens channels through which God's healing Spirit flows." How have you seen this in your experience?

4. Reread the Beatitudes, and discuss where you fit into them (e.g., are you poor in spirit, meek, mourning, etc.?). Then discuss Jesus' promise to those who are feeling what you are feeling.

TRY THIS!

Take to heart Dr. Wilson's challenge to turn your attention away from yourself. Choose someone or some task that could benefit from your help, and pour yourself into that project.